VERBAL ART AS PERFORMANCE

Richard Bauman
The University of Texas at Austin

With supplementary essays by:
Barbara A. Babcock
Gary H. Gossen
Roger D. Abrahams
Joel F. Sherzer

WAVELAND

PRESS, INC.

Prospect Heights, Illinois

For information about this book, write or call:
Waveland Press, Inc.
P.O. Box 400
Prospect Heights, Illinois 60070
(708) 634-0081

Printed in the United States of America

10 9 8 7

CONTENTS

ACKNOWLEDGMENTS

In the development of the ideas presented in this work I have profited greatly from discussions with many colleagues and students over the past several years. Among those who deserve special mention and thanks are Barbara Babcock, Dan Ben-Amos, Marcia Herndon, Barbara Kirshenblatt-Gimblett, John McDowell, Norma McLeod, Américo Paredes, Dina Sherzer, and Beverly Stoeltje. Thanks are also due to Keith Basso for his comments and encouragement in the writing of an earlier version of this work. My greatest debt, however, is to the three individuals who have stimulated and influenced my thinking most profoundly: Dell Hymes, for imparting to me the ethnographic perspective on verbal art and for his ideas on the nature of performance; Roger D. Abrahams, for focusing my attention on performance as an organizing principle for the study of folklore; and Joel Sherzer for sharing in the intellectual process all along the way. Finally, sincere thanks once again to Frances Terry for her meticulous care in producing the succession of manuscripts that culminated in this book.

PREFACE

The essay which constitutes the first half of this book is a considerably expanded version of the author's earlier work, "Verbal Art as Performance," which appeared in the *American Anthropologist,* vol. 77 (1975), pp. 290-311. The supplementary essays have been included because they deal in depth with aspects of the argument presented in the title essay, presenting further illustrative data, and suggesting further and more detailed applications and ramifications of central ideas. Two of the articles, by Barbara Babcock and Joel F. Sherzer, are original contributions, published here for the first time; the essays by Roger D. Abrahams and Gary H. Gossen are reprinted here from other sources.

Verbal Art as Performance is written from the perspective of the folklorist and linguistic anthropologist, but it owes much as well to my earlier training in literature. Because my commitments are fundamentally interdisciplinary, I have been gratified to learn that the original essay has been of interest and use to scholars and students in a range of other fields beyond these, including linguistics, speech, and fine arts. The present volume has been assembled to maintain the interdisciplinary thrust of the earlier work; the authors of the various essays come from folklore, anthropology, linguistics, and literature, but all share a fundamental interest in the esthetic dimension of human existence. This volume is intended as a contribution to the study and appreciation of artistic action in social life, from any of the disciplinary vantage points that bear upon this interest and that share the belief that it is, in fact, performance that counts.

FOREWORD

The cross-disciplinary and integrative nature of sociolinguistics is clearly evidenced in the work of Richard Bauman. In this volume he brings together folklore, anthropology, linguistics and literary criticism as they focus on verbal art. A concern for language in use has gradually emerged in recent years. Philosophers of language speak about how to get things done with words. Linguists seek to understand implicature in language. Literary critics seek to understand intentionality, motivation and point of view. Anthropologists seek to discover the systematic patterning of such events as illustrative of culture. The work represented here is a clear assembly of perspectives and methodology of these fields from the viewpoint of performance—artistic action and artistic event. The basic principles underlying sociolinguistics (patterned variability and context as revealed through language) provide the coherence.

In addition to Bauman's conceptual framework, this book brings together supplementary essays which clarify, illustrate and amplify in a pioneering effort to treat verbal art as performance. Especially important are the detailed treatments of metanarration, genres, talk about talk and ritual speaking events. The examples selected are from a variety of languages and cultures offering the usual anthropological depth but within a conceptually manageable frame of reference. It represents an important beginning of what we hope will be a productive avenue of study in the future.

Roger W. Shuy

Georgetown University
Center for Applied Linguistics
June 1977

VERBAL ART AS PERFORMANCE

Richard Bauman

PART I

1

INTRODUCTION

We will be concerned in this work to develop a conception of verbal art as performance, based upon an understanding of performance as a mode of speaking. In constructing this framework for a performance-centered approach to verbal art, we have started from the position of the folklorist but have drawn from a wide range of disciplines, chiefly anthropology, linguistics, and literary criticism. Each of these disciplines has its own distinctive perspective on verbal art, and a long tradition of independent scholarship in its study. From at least the time of Herder, however, there has been an integrative tradition as well in the study of verbal art, manifested in the work of such figures as Edward Sapir, Roman Jakobson, and Dell Hymes—scholars who have operated at an intellectual level beyond the boundaries which separate academic disciplines, sharing an interest in the esthetic dimension of social and cultural life in human communities as manifested through the use of language. The

3

present work is offered in the spirit of that integrative tradition.

In recent years, the concept of performance has begun to assume central importance in the orientation of increasing numbers of folklorists and others interested in verbal art.[1] As employed in the work of these scholars, the term "performance" has been used to convey a dual sense of artistic *action*—the doing of folklore—and artistic *event*—the performance situation, involving performer, art form, audience, and setting—both of which are basic to the developing performance approach. This usage accords well with the conventional meaning of the term "performance" and has served to point up the fundamental reorientation from folklore-as-materials to folklore-as-communication which characterized the thinking of these scholars. Conventional meanings can carry scholarship just so far, however, before the lack of conceptual rigor begins to constrain analytical insight rather than advancing it. In view of the centrality of performance to the orientation of increasing numbers of folklorists and anthropologists interested in verbal art, the time seems opportune for efforts aimed at expanding the conceptual content of folkloric performance as a communicative phenomenon, beyond the general usage that has carried us up to this point. That is the purpose of this work.

One orientational and terminological point before proceeding: consistent with the chiefly sociolinguistic and anthropological roots of the performance approach, the terms "verbal art" and "oral literature" provide a better frame of reference, at least as a point of departure for the ideas to be advanced here, than the more diffuse and problematic term "folklore." "Spoken art" might be even better, insofar as this essay is concerned solely with a way of speaking and its attendant phenomena, but the term has never achieved currency in any of the disciplines where it might have served a useful purpose—folklore, anthropology, or linguistics.[2] Many things have been studied under the name of folklore, but verbal art has always been at or near the center of the larger domain and has constituted the chief common ground between anthropological folklorists and those of other persuasions. Accordingly, the shift from the "folklore" of the preceding paragraph to the "verbal art" of those to follow is neither unprecedented nor arbitrary but will serve to make somewhat clearer the universe of discourse within which the ideas which follow have been formulated.

Let us make explicit as well that a great deal more is intended here than a convenient relabeling of what is already known. The conception of performance to be developed in these pages is not simply an alternative perspective on the familiar genres of oral literature long studied by folklorists and anthropologists. It is that; but it is more than that as well. Performance, as we conceive of it and as our examples have been selected to illustrate, is a unifying thread tying together the marked, segregated esthetic genres and other spheres of verbal behavior into a general unified conception of verbal art as a way of speaking. Verbal art may comprehend both myth narration and the speech expected of certain members of society whenever they open their mouths, and it is performance that brings them together in culture-specific and variable ways, ways that are to be discovered ethnographically within each culture and community.

2

THE NATURE OF PERFORMANCE

Modern theories of the nature of verbal art, whether in anthropology, linguistics, or literature, tend overwhelmingly to be constructed in terms of special usages or patterning of formal features within texts. General formulations identify a primary "focus on the message for its own sake" (Jakobson 1960:356, Stankiewicz 1960:14-15) or a "concern with the form of expression, over and above the needs of communication" (Bascom 1955:247) as the essence of verbal art. Others are more specific about the nature or consequences of such a focus or concern, suggesting, for example, that the touchstone of verbal art lies in a maximized "use of the devices of the language in such a way that this use itself attracts attention and is perceived as uncommon" (Havránek 1964:10). Among certain linguists, the idea has some currency that verbal art "in some way deviates from norms which we, as members of society, have learnt to expect in the medium used" (Leech 1969:56, cf. Stankiewicz 1960:12, Durbin 1971), while others of their colleagues make a point of the "multiplicity of *additional formal laws* restricting the poet's free choice of expressions" (Fónagy 1965:72, italics in the original).

Whatever their differences, of focus or emphasis, all these approaches make for a conception of verbal art that is text-centered. For all, the artful, esthetic quality of an utterance resides in the way in which language is used in the construction of the textual item. To be sure, it may be considered necessary, at least implicitly, to assess the text against the background of general linguistic norms, but it is the text itself that remains the unit of analysis and point of departure for proponents of these approaches. This in turn places severe constraints on the development of a meaningful framework for the understanding of verbal art as performance, as a species of situated human communication, a way of speaking.

It is, of course, possible to move from artistic texts, identified in formal or other terms, to performance, by simply looking at how such texts are rendered, in action terms. But this is to proceed backwards, by approaching phenomena whose primary social reality lies in their nature as oral communication in terms of the abstracted textual products of the communicative process. As we shall see, oral literary texts, though they may fulfill the formal measures of verbal art, be accurately recorded, and bear strong associations with performance in their conventional contexts, may nevertheless not be the products of performance, but of rendition in another communicative mode. How many of the texts in our collections represent recordings of informants' abstracts, résumés, or reports of performance and performance forms rather than true performances (cf. Tedlock 1972a)? By identifying the nature of performance and distinguishing it from other ways of speaking, we will have, among other things, a measure of the authenticity of collected oral literary texts.

A performance-centered conception of verbal art calls for an approach through performance itself. In such an approach, the formal manipulation of linguistic features is secondary to the nature of performance, per se, conceived of and defined as a mode of communication.

There is a very old conception of verbal art as communication which goes back at least to Plato's insistence that literature is lies. This notion, also manifest in Sir Philip Sidney's dictum, "the poet nothing affirmeth" (Ohmann 1971:5), holds that whatever the propositional content of an item of verbal art, its meaning is somehow canceled out or rendered inoperative by the nature of the utterance as verbal art. A more recent expression of this conception is to be found in the writings of the British Ordinary Language philosopher, J. L. Austin. Austin maintains, "of any and every utterance," that it will be "*in a peculiar way* hollow or void if said by an actor on the stage . . . or spoken in soliloquy." He continues, "language in such circumstances is in special ways— intelligibly—used not seriously, but in ways *parasitic* upon its normal use—ways which fall under the doctrine of *etiolations* of language" (Austin 1962:21-22, italics in the original).[1]

Leaving aside the unfortunate suggestion that the uses Austin mentions exert a weakening influence on language, a product of his particular bias, we may abstract from the cited passage the suggestion that performance represents a transformation of the basic referential ("serious," "normal" in Austin's terms) uses of language. In other words, in artistic performance of this kind, there is something going on in the communicative interchange which says to the auditor, "interpret what I say in some special sense; do not take it to mean what the words alone, taken literally, would convey." This may lead to the further suggestion that performance sets up, or represents, an interpretative frame within which the messages being communicated are to be understood, and that this frame contrasts with at least one other frame, the literal.

In employing the term "frame" here, I am drawing not upon Austin, but on the powerful insights of Gregory Bateson and the more recent and equally provocative work of Erving Goffman (1974). Bateson first developed systematically the notion of frame as a defined interpretive context providing guidelines for discriminating between orders of message (1972

[1956] :222), in his seminal article, "A Theory of Play and Fantasy" (1972 [1955] :177-93). We shall return to aspects of this theory and of Goffman's in more detail below.[2]

Although the notion of performance as a frame was introduced above as contrasting with literal communication, it should be made clear from the beginning that many other such frames besides these two may be identified. For example:

insinuation, in which the words spoken are to be interpreted as having a covert and indirect relation to the meaning of the utterance (cf. Austin 1962:121);

joking, in which the words spoken are to be interpreted as not seriously meaning what they might otherwise mean (cf. Austin 1962:121);

imitation, in which the manner of speaking is to be interpreted as being modeled after that of another person or persons;

translation, in which the words spoken are to be interpreted as the equivalent of words originally spoken in another language or code;

quotation, in which the words spoken are to be interpreted as the words of someone other than the speaker (cf. Weinreich 1966:162).

This is a very partial and unelaborated list, which does not even adequately sample, much less exhaust, the range of possible interpretive frames within which communication may occur. It should be noted, moreover, that frames may be used in combination, as well as singly, as listed. It should also be stressed that although theorists like Austin suggest that the literal frame somehow has priority over all the others—is more "normal"—this is not necessary to the theory and in fact biases it in unproductive ways (Fish 1973). The notorious difficulty of defining literalness aside, there is growing evidence that literal utterances are no more frequent or "normal" in situated human communication than any of the other frames, and indeed that in spoken communication no such thing as naked literalness may actually exist (Burns 1972, Goffman 1974). For our purposes, all that is necessary is the recognition of performance as a distinctive frame, available as a communicative resource along with the others to speakers in particular communities.[3]

The first major task, then, is to suggest what kind of interpretive frame performance establishes or represents. How is communication that constitutes performance to be interpreted? The following represents a very preliminary attempt to specify the interpretive guidelines set up by the performance frame.

Fundamentally, performance as a mode of spoken verbal communication consists in the assumption of responsibility to an audience for a display of communicative competence. This competence rests on the knowledge and ability to speak in socially appropriate ways. Performance involves on the part of the performer an assumption of accountability to an audience for the way in which communication is carried out, above and beyond its referential content. From the point of view of the audience, the act of expression on the part of the performer is thus marked as subject to evaluation for the way it is done, for the relative skill and effectiveness of the performer's display of competence.[4] Additionally, it is marked as available for the enhancement of experience, through the present enjoyment of the intrinsic qualities of the act of expression itself. Performance thus calls forth special attention to and heightened awareness of the act of expression and gives license to the audience to regard the act of expression and the performer with special intensity.[5]

Thus conceived, performance is a mode of language use, a way of speaking. The implication of such a concept for a theory of verbal art is this: it is no longer necessary to begin with artful texts, identified on independent formal grounds and then reinjected into situations of use, in order to conceptualize verbal art in communicative terms. Rather, in terms of the approach being developed here, performance becomes *constitutive* of the domain of verbal art as spoken communication.

Some examples may be useful at this point, to demonstrate in empirical terms the application of the notion of performance we have proposed. In several of her writings on the people of the plateau area of the Malagasy Republic (Keenan 1973, 1974), Elinor Keenan delineates the two major ways of speaking identified by this group. The first, called in native terminology, *resaka,* may be loosely defined as informal conversation, described by native elders as "everyday talk," or "simple talk." The other way of speaking, *kabary,* is the one of principal interest to us here. *Kabary* is glossed by Keenan as "ceremonial speech, what we might call oratory." The following are excerpts from Keenan's description:

> *Kabary* is a focal point of tradition and as a focal point of artistic expression is . . . regarded with great interest. It is not uncommon to see groups of elders evaluating the skills and approaches of speechmakers following a *kabary* performance. A speechmaker who pleases his audience is rewarded with praise such as: "He is a very sharp speechmaker." "He is prepared." "He is a true speechmaker, a child of his father." His words are said to be "well-arranged" and "balanced." His performance is described as "satisfying." . . . Evaluations are based on both skill in handling winding speech and on one's ability to follow certain rules governing the sequence and content of particular oratory. (1973:226-27)

And further, "*kabary* performances . . . are platforms for exhibiting knowledge of traditional oratory" (1973:229). Wedding *kabary,* in particular, "is the most developed art form in the culture and a source of great delight and interest to all participants" (1973:242).

It is clear from this description that *kabary* represents for the plateau Malagasy a domain of performance. To engage in *kabary* is to assume responsibility to one's audience for a display of competence in the traditional *kabary* forms, to render one's speech subject to evaluation for the quality of one's speaking. One is judged as a speechmaker, for the way one's words are arranged. *Kabary* performances are keenly attended to and actively evaluated, with good performances serving as a source of enjoyment and satisfaction to the auditors, for the way they are done. The ethnography of verbal art among the plateau Malagasy thus becomes centrally the ethnography of *kabary.*

Among the Ilongot of the Philippines, by contrast with the above, there are three major speech styles, described by

Michelle Rosaldo: the stylistically unmarked "straight speech" (*qube:nata qupu*), invocatory speech (*nawnaw*), and a third style, *qambaqan*, described as "crooked" or witty talk (Rosaldo 1973). It is not wholly clear from Rosaldo's account whether *nawnaw* involves performance, but *qambaqan* very clearly does. *Qambaqan* is "artful, witty, charming," "a language of display, performance, pose" (Rosaldo 1973:197-98). What is especially noteworthy about speaking among the Ilongot, within our present context, is that the telling of tales, always included in a priori text-centered definitions of verbal art, is classified as a kind of "straight speech." That is, storytelling for the Ilongot is not a form of performance and thus, in culture-specific communicative terms, not a form of verbal art. The domain of speaking among the Ilongot is to this extent, among many others, organized differently from that of the many cultures in which storytelling does involve performance.

Japanese professional storytellers, for example, as described by Hrdličková, are certainly performers in our sense of the term. For their audiences, "it is not seldom more important *how* a story is told than *what* the story relates. . . . Storytellers regard the mastery of [storytelling] elements as a necessary preliminary stage prior to any successful practicing of their art in public, since the audience not only expects of them an established manner of interpretation, but also rates them according to the degree of artistry the artists command" (Hrdličková 1969:193, italics in the original). That is, storytelling involves a display of competence in the manner of telling the story, which is subject to evaluation for the way it is done. The audience derives enjoyment from the performance in proportion to the skill of the narrator (*Idem.*).

The point to be emphasized here is that just as speaking itself as a cultural system (or as part of cultural systems defined in other terms) will vary from speech community to speech community, so too will the nature and extent of the realm of performance and verbal art (Bauman 1972). One of the principal questions one must ask in the ethnography of performance is what range of speech activity is regarded as susceptible to performance and what range is conventionally performed, that is, conventionally expected by members of the community to be rendered in a performance mode.[6] For the St. Vincentians, for example, performance may be invoked across a very wide spectrum of speech activity, from oratory, to storytelling, to gossip—even to speaking with a speech impediment—while the seventeenth-century Quakers, because of basic attitudes toward speaking in general, restricted performance to an extremely narrow range of activity (Abrahams 1970a, Abrahams and Bauman 1971, Bauman 1974, 1975). In performance terms, it is not possible to assert a priori that verbal art consists of "folktales, myths, legends, proverbs, riddles, and other literary forms" defined solely in formal terms (Bascom 1955:245). We will return to the culture-specific nature of verbal art as performance below.

3

THE KEYING OF PERFORMANCE

Before embarking upon a discussion of the further implications of the notion of performance put forward above, there is one major element integral to the conception of performance as a frame which must be delineated, i.e., the way in which framing is accomplished, or, to use Goffman's term for the process by which frames are invoked and shifted, how performance is *keyed* (Goffman 1974). Here again, we may draw on Bateson's powerful insight, that it is characteristic of communicative interaction that it include a range of explicit or implicit messages which carry instructions on how to interpret the other message(s) being communicated. This communication about communication Bateson termed metacommunication (Ruesch and Bateson 1968:209). In Bateson's terms, "a frame is metacommunicative. Any message, which either explicitly or implicitly defines a frame, *ipso facto* gives the receiver instructions or aids in his attempt to understand the messages included within the frame" (Bateson 1972

[1955] :188). All framing, then, including performance, is accomplished through the employment of culturally conventionalized metacommunication. In empirical terms, this means that each speech community will make use of a structured set of distinctive communicative means from among its resources in culturally conventionalized and culture-specific ways to key the performance frame, such that all communication that takes place within that frame is to be understood as performance within that community.

A general list of communicative means that have been widely documented in various cultures as serving to key performance is not difficult to compile. Such a list would include at least the following:

    special codes;
    figurative language;
    parallelism;
    special paralinguistic features;
    special formulae;
    appeal to tradition;
    disclaimer of performance.

The formal and conventional nature of most of these devices bears an important relation to the very nature of performance itself. Burke has alerted us to the power of formal patterns to elicit the participation of an audience through the arousal of "an attitude of collaborative expectancy. . . . Once you grasp the trend of the form, it invites participation." This "yielding to the formal development, surrendering to its symmetry as such" (Burke 1969 [1950] :58), fixes the attention of the audience more strongly on the performer, binds the audience to the performer in a relationship of dependence that keeps them caught up in his display. A not insignificant part of the capacity of performance to transform social structure, to be discussed at the end of this work, resides in the power that the performer derives from the control over his audience afforded him by the formal appeal of his performance.

Let us examine the devices we have listed at greater length.

Special codes. The use of special codes is one of the most widely noted characteristics of verbal art, so much so that special linguistic usage is taken often as a definitive criterion of poetic language. The special usage may center on one or another linguistic level or features, or it may extend to whole codes.

Not infrequently, there is an attribution of archaism to the special language of verbal art, a natural outgrowth of the traditionality and esotericism of many performance systems. Such attribution need not imply unintelligibility, however; Navajo usage is a case in point. Informants identify the special language of storytelling as "old-fashioned" (Toelken 1969:220), but it is readily understood by all, even children. From a purely functional point of view, of course, such usages are no more archaic than the language of everyday speech, insofar as they have a vital—if restricted—place in contemporary speaking.

There is a major theoretical point here. Much discussion of the nature of verbal art is founded on the notion that it is part of the essence of poetic language that it is somehow deviant from normal language (see above (pp. 7-10). Normal language, in these formulations turns out to be literal, strictly referential "standard" language. We have discussed this perspective earlier, in connection with J. L. Austin. The ethnographic perspective employed in this work is fundamentally at odds with the deviationist perspective. It rests instead on a multifunctional view of language use, which recognizes that the members of every speech community have available to them a diversity of linguistic means of speaking, none of which can serve a priori as an analytical frame of reference for any other. We can thus speak appropriately of difference among registers or varieties within a community, but not deviance.

Figurative language. No single feature or device figures more consistently or prominently in accounts of the characteristics of verbal art than figurative language. The semantic density of figurative language, its foregroundedness, make it especially appropriate as a device for performance, where expressive intensity and special communicative skill are central. The nature of figurative expression is so complex and extensive a subject that it is impossible even to suggest all the relevant dimensions here. (For a fuller discussion, see Fernandez 1974.)

Nevertheless, one important element of contrast in the role that figurative language assumes in artistic verbal performance should be addressed, namely, the creativity of the performer vis-à-vis the figures he employs. In some communities, the coinage of original figures is what is valued. For the Western Apache, for example, the coinage of metaphorical "wise words" in the course of conversation is itself a form of performance in every sense of the term (Basso 1976). On the other hand, the prominence of traditional fixed-phrase performance forms in the performance economies of the world's communities is also amply documented. Figurative language is no less important in such traditional forms; performance may thus consist in the accurate rendition of ready made figures. To cite but one of a myriad of possible examples, the panegyric poetry of Ruanda, heavily figurative in expression, is performed with special attention to exactness of wording (Finnegan 1970:118). There is, finally, a third alternative, namely, that the figures employed by the performer may be ready made, but that performance involves their employment in novel contexts. The use of metaphor in Homeric epic is a case in point. Homer's metaphors, as Parry has demonstrated, are traditional and formulaic, their very ready-madeness essential to the formulaic improvisation of the oral epic performance (Parry 1933).

Parallelism. Parallelism, what Leech calls "foregrounded regularity" (1969:62), involves the repetition, with systematic variation, of phonic, grammatical, semantic, or prosodic structures, the combination of invariant and variant elements in the construction of an utterance (Jakobson 1966, 1968; Austerlitz 1960). From a functional point of view, the persistence of the invariant elements and the structural principles underlying the parallel constructions may serve as mnemonic aids to the performer of a fixed traditional text, or enhance the fluency of the improvisational or spontaneous performance. In either case, the fluent use of language marked by extra regularities is an effective vehicle for the display of communicative competence.

Parallelism is so fundamental and universal a phenomenon that Jakobson, to whom is owed much of the current interest in parallelism, suggests that it is "the empirical linguistic criterion of the poetic function" (Jakobson 1960:358). However, parallelism has been studied almost exclusively as it figures in highly marked and elaborate systems of oral poetry, such as oral epic or ritual speech (for ethnographic examples, see Bricker 1974; Fox 1974; Gossen 1972, 1974a, 1974b; Sherzer and Sherzer 1972), with little or no attention to its use as an esthetic device in conversational contexts. From the perspective we have been developing here, however, the capacity of parallelism to extend from brief passing utterances to lengthy and elaborate poetic forms is an important factor, because it gives us a clue to potential continuities between elaborate, scheduled, public performances, involving highly marked performance forms, and other contexts for discourse in which performance may be more fleeting and transitory. For example, the performance motive in contemporary urban Afro-American culture, illuminated by Roger Abrahams (1970b), is manifested in clichés, brief leavetaking formulas, the rhymed dozens (a form of verbal dueling), the epic toasts, and the religious sermons (Rosenberg 1970) of male performers in this community; all these forms—from short and conversational to elaborate and highly marked—are suffused with parallelistic constructions.

Special paralinguistic features. Paralinguistic features, by their very nature, tend not to be captured in the transcribed or published versions of texts, with the exception of certain aspects of prosody in clearly poetic forms. The reader is consequently forced to rely on the incidental comments of the occasional sensitive observer who does note paralinguistic features of delivery style. These will generally take the form of descriptive notes, such as, "the Mohave have a traditional staccato, strongly accented and rather rapid manner of

delivering traditional memorized texts" (Devereux 1949:269).
It is not only that recorded texts do not readily reflect
paralinguistic features, but that in many cases, especially
before the ready availability of tape recorders, the conditions
of recording artistic texts *required* that conventional
paralinguistic patterns be distorted, with what resultant effects
on the text it is difficult to determine. The Mohave style noted
by Devereux, for example, made it impossible to record
conventionally performed texts by hand; consequently
Devereux insisted that his informants slow down their delivery
to a pace that allowed him to take down what they said. Were
these latter renditions performances? Certainly not by full
Mohave standards.

A major step toward rectifying the omission of
paralinguistic features of narrative performance has been taken
by Dennis Tedlock, in his work on Zuñi narrative (Tedlock
1972a, 1972b). Tedlock has developed a series of conventions
for indicating such features as rate, length, pause duration,
pitch contour, tone of voice, loudness, and stress, that seem
relatively simple and straightforward but are revolutionary in
conception. Tedlock's method not only makes it possible to
transcribe performed texts in a way that reveals crucial
features that mark it as the product of performance, but
points the way to a fundamental reorientation in our conception of what constitutes an adequate text.

John McDowell (1974) has recently made a significant
contribution toward establishing the importance of paralinguistic features as keys to performance, while underscoring the
distinctiveness of performance as a way of speaking.
Comparing two renditions in Bolivian Quechua of the same
tale by the same narrator, one a report of the tale's content,
the other a performance, McDowell discovered virtually total
contrast in paralinguistic features between the two. The
constellation of paralinguistic features keying performance in
Bolivian Quechua, however, is not necessarily the same as one
would find in another community; what is important is the
contrast between performance and other ways of speaking in
the informant's own community.

Special formulae. Very familiar to English-speaking audiences are formulae such as, "once upon a time," opening a fairy tale, or "did you hear the one about . . . ," to introduce a joke (cf. Reaver 1972). Such formulae are, in effect, markers of specific genres, and insofar as these genres are conventionally performed in a community, the formulae may serve as keys to performance.

The formulae may be of several types. The Bahamian "Bunday," for example, has no currency or meaning except as a marker of traditional folktales, or "old stories." To the Bahamians, "Bunday ain't nothing, it just mean is old story" (Crowley 1966:20). Alternatively, the formula may be a naming of the genre itself, as in the Clackamas Chinook ending, "myth myth" (Jacobs 1959:221). A third possibility is a formula that performs some referential function, however conventional, for the item itself, as in "once upon a time," which places the action of a folktale in the past. Finally, the formula may refer to the communicative relationship between performer and audience, as in "did you hear the one about . . . ?" (The fullest discussion of this entire phenomenon is in Babcock this volume).

Appeal to tradition. To assume responsibility for the way in which one carries out a communicative act implies a standard of judgment against which one's performance is to be evaluated. There are esthetic standards brought to bear here, having to do with the intrinsic qualities of the act of expression itself, but there may also be an appeal to tradition, the acceptance of past practice as a standard of reference. In tradition-oriented societies, an appeal to tradition may thus become a key to performance, a way of signaling the assumption of responsibility for the proper doing of a communicative act. In the words of the Mandinka griot,

> What I have myself heard,
> What I have heard from my parents,
> That is the account which I shall put before you. (Innes 1974:145)

Disclaimer of performance. Finally, we must note that the conventional means used to announce performance may amount to a surface denial of any real competence at all, a kind of disclaimer of performance. This is true, for instance, among the plateau Malagasy, for whom the elaborate assertion of verbal incompetence is a diagnostic feature of *kabary* performance (Keenan 1974:135). Likewise, the traditional Cree storyteller opened his performance with a denial of personal competence (Darnell 1974:325). Such disclaimers are not, of course, incompatible with taking responsibility for a display of competence, but are, rather, concessions to standards of etiquette and decorum, where self-assertiveness is disvalued. In such situations, a disclaimer of performance serves both as a moral gesture, to counterbalance the power of performance to focus heightened attention on the performer, and a key to performance itself.

A list of the kind just given is ultimately of only limited utility, for the essential task in the ethnography of performance is to determine *the culture-specific constellations of communicative means that serve to key performance in particular communities.* Features such as those listed above may figure in a variety of ways in the speech economy of a community. Rhyme, for example, may be used to key performance, or it may simply be a formal feature of the language, as when it figures in certain forms of reduplication, or it may appear in speech play (which may or may not involve performance). It may even be inadvertent. Interestingly, when this happens in English, there is a traditional formula which may be invoked to disclaim performance retroactively: "I'm a poet and I don't know it; my feet show it, they're longfellows." This is an indication that rhyme often does in fact key performance in English.

The basic point here is that one must determine empirically what are the specific conventionalized means that key performance in a particular community, and that these will vary from one community to another though one may discover areal and typological patterns (Jacobs 1972, Sherzer and Bauman 1972:145-47), and universal tendencies may exist. A full and ideal ethnography of performance would indicate the keys to the entire domain, viewing speaking and performance as a cultural system and indicating how the whole range of performance is keyed. Gary Gossen's elegant analyses of Chamula genres of verbal behavior comes closest to any work in the literature known to the author in achieving such a description (Gossen 1972 reprinted this volume, 1974a, 1974b). Within the overall domain of "people's speech" (*sk'op kirsano*), Chamula identify three macrocategories of speech: "ordinary speech" (*lo?il k'op*), "speech for people whose hearts are heated" (*k'op sventa sk'isnah yo?nton yu?un li kirsanoe*), and "pure speech" (*puru k'op*). Ordinary speech is conceived of by the people as unmarked, not special in any way. It is not associated with performance. Speech for people whose hearts are heated and pure speech, on the other hand, are strongly relevant to our discussion.

As an overall category, what distinguishes speech for people whose hearts are heated from ordinary speech is that it is stylistically marked by a degree of verbatim repetition of words, phrases, and metaphors, and in certain subcategories, or genres, by parallelism in syntax and metaphorical couplets. Pure speech is distinguished in turn from speech for people whose hearts are heated by its relative fixity of form and the greater density of parallelism, either through proliferation of syntactically parallel lines or the "stacking" of metaphorical couplets.

From Gossen's description, it is evident that repetition and parallelism constitute keys to performance for the Chamula. Both speech for people whose hearts are heated and pure speech involve the display of competence, contribute to the enhancement of experience, and are subject to evaluation for the way they are done. There is a crucial point to be made here, however. Speech for people whose hearts are heated is idiosyncratic, unfixed, and markedly less saturated with those features that signal performance. The user of speech for people whose hearts are heated is less fully accountable for a display of competence, his expression is less intensely regarded by the audience, his performance has less to contribute to the enhancement of the audience's experience than the one who uses the forms of pure speech. The performance frame may thus be seen to operate with variable intensity in Chamula speaking.

It is worth underscoring this last point. Art is commonly conceived as an all-or-nothing phenomenon—something either is or is not art—but conceived as performance, in terms of an interpretive frame, verbal art may be culturally defined as varying in intensity as well as range. We are not speaking here of the relative quality of a performance—good performance vs. bad performance—but the degree of intensity with which the performance frame operates in a particular range of culturally defined ways of speaking. When we move beyond the first-level discrimination of culturally-defined ways of speaking that do not conventionally involve performance (e.g., Chamula ordinary speech, Malagasy *resaka*) vs. ways of speaking that do characteristically involve performance (e.g., Chamula speech for people whose hearts are heated and pure speech, Malagasy *kabary*), we need to attend to the relative saturation of the performance frame attendant upon the more specific categories of ways of speaking within the community.

The variable range of performance in Chamula is confirmed by the metalanguage employed by the Chamula in their evaluation of performance. Because of the importance of the evaluative dimension of performance as communication, such metalanguages and the esthetic standards they express constitute an essential consideration in the ethnography of performance; the range of application of such esthetic systems may be the best indicator of the extent of the performance domain within a community (Dundes 1966, Babcock this volume; Foster 1974a:32-35). Increased fixity of form, repetition, and parallelism, which serve as measures of increasing intensity of performance, also signal for the Chamula increasing "heat." Heat is a basic metaphor for the Chamula, symbolizing the orderly, the good, and the beautiful, by derivation from the power of the sun deity. The transition from ordinary speech to speech for people whose hearts are heated to pure speech thus involves a progressive increase in heat and therefore of esthetic and ethical value in speaking.

4

THE PATTERNING OF PERFORMANCE

Our discussion of Chamula performance at the close of the last chapter centered upon the way in which performance is keyed, the communicative means that signal that a particular act of expression is being performed. We may advance our considerations still further by recognizing that it is only as these means are embodied in particular genres that they figure in the performance system of the Chamula themselves. That is, the Chamula organize the domain of speaking in terms of genres, i.e., culturally definable, traditional types of verbal communication (Enkvist 1973:20), conventionalized utterance types that incorporate the features that key performance. Thus, terms such as *k'op sventa cavilto* "court speech," *baȼ'i ?ac' k'op* "true recent narrative," and *?antivo k'opetik* "ancient words" designate specific Chamula genres. The association of performance with particular genres is a significant aspect of the patterning of performance within communities. This association is more problematic than text-centered, etic approaches to verbal art would indicate (Ben-Amos 1969).

In the ethnography of performance as a cultural system, the investigator's attention will frequently be attracted first by those genres that are conventionally performed. These are the genres, like the Chamula genres of pure speech or Bahamian old stories, for which there is little or no expectation on the part of members of the community that they will be rendered in any other way. He should be attentive as well, however, for those genres for which the expectation or probability of performance is lower, for which performance is felt to be more optional, but which occasion no surprise if they are performed. A familiar example from contemporary American society might be the personal narrative, which is frequently rendered in a simply repertorial mode, but which may well be highlighted as performance. Labov's sophisticated research on personal narrative suggests that one of the principal factors entering into the rendering of personal narrative as performance, and determining its effectiveness as performance, is the inclusion in the narrative of an evaluative component that indicates the nature and intensity of the narrator's feelings concerning the experience he is recounting—why he considers it worth telling about (Labov 1972a:354-96).

There will, of course, in any society, be a range of verbal genres that are not rendered as performances. These will be viewed as not involving the kind of competence that is susceptible to display, not lending themselves to the enhancement of experience. Not to be forgotten are those genres that are considered by members of the community to be performance forms, but that are nevertheless not performed, as when there is no one left who is competent to perform them, or conditions for appropriate performance no longer exist. A related phenomenon is what Hymes (personal communication) calls performance in a perfunctory key, in which the responsibility for a display of communicative competence is undertaken out of a sense of cultural duty, traditional obligation, but offering, because of changed circumstances, relatively little pleasure or enhancement of experience. One thinks, for example, of some masses in Latin. Such performances may, however, be a means of preserving performance forms for later reinvigoration and restoration to the level of full performance.

It should be noted, with reference to the native organization of the domain of speaking and cultural expectations for performance, that the members of a community may conceptualize speech activity in terms of acts rather than genres. The St. Vincentians are a case in point: representative St. Vincentian speech acts susceptible to performance are *giving fatigue, making melée, telling story* (Abrahams and Bauman 1971). Speech acts and genres are, of course, analytically distinct, the former having to do with speech behavior, the latter with the verbal products of that behavior. For an oral culture, however, the distinction may not be significant, if it is recognized at all. Thus a particular performance system may well be organized by members of the community in terms of speech acts that conventionally involve performance, others that may or may not, and still others for which performance is not a relevant consideration.

We view the act of performance as situated behavior, situated within and rendered meaningful with reference to relevant contexts. Such contexts may be identified at a variety of levels—in terms of settings, for example, the culturally defined places where performance occurs. Institutions too—religion, education, politics—may be viewed from the perspective of the way in which they do or do not represent contexts for performance within communities. Most important as an organizing principle in the ethnography of performance is the event (or scene) within which performance occurs (see, e.g., Kirshenblatt-Gimblett 1974). We use the term "event" to designate a culturally defined, bounded segment of the flow of behavior and experience constituting a meaningful context for action (cf. Frake 1964, Hymes 1967, 1972).[1]

There are, first of all, events for which performance is required, for which it is a criterial attribute, such that performance is a necessary component for a particular event to count as a valid instance of the class. These will be what Singer calls "cultural performances" (Singer 1972:71). They may be organized and conducted primarily for entertainment, such as Bahamian old story sessions, or Vincentian tea meetings, or they may have some other stated primary purpose, like Malagasy bride-price meetings, but performance will be as. integral a component for the latter as for the former. As with genres and acts, there are other events for which performance is an optional feature, not necessary or invariably expected, but not unexpected or surprising, as when someone tells jokes at a party. Again, there will be a further range of events in which performance is extraneous, not a relevant variable insofar as people categorize and participate in the events of their culture.

Cultural performances tend to be the most prominent performance contexts within a community. They are, as a rule, scheduled events, restricted in setting, clearly bounded, and widely public, involving the most highly formalized perform-ance forms and accomplished performers of the community. Because they are scheduled, public, and elaborate, these performances are especially attractive and interesting to ethnographers. This makes it all the more necessary to reassert that these factors are not intrinsic to performance as conceptualized in this work. As interesting as cultural performances are, performance occurs outside of them as well, and the most challenging job that faces the student of performance is establishing the continuity between the noticeable and public performance of cultural performances, and the spontaneous, unscheduled, optional performance contexts of everyday life.

The structure of performance events is a product of the interplay of many factors, including setting, act sequence, and ground rules of performance. These last will consist of the set of cultural themes and ethical and social-interactional organizing principles that govern the conduct of performance (Bauman and Sherzer 1974: Section III). As a kind of speaking, performance will be subject to a range of community ground rules that regulate speaking in general (Bauman 1975), but there will also be a set of ground rules specific to performance itself, for example, the Wishram requirement that members of the audience periodically signal their attentiveness to a myth performance (Hymes 1966:149), or the obligation of the Iroquois speaker to refrain from intruding a personal element into ritual speeches, in which he acts as spokesman for a group (Foster 1974b:364). It is important to be aware, however, that ethics and esthetics are not always as coterminous as Gossen suggests, in his analysis of Chamula ways of speaking. In St. Vincent, for example, the domain "talking nonsense" is negatively valued in terms of ethics but encompasses a range of speech activities with a strong performance element about them that is highly valued and much enjoyed in esthetic terms (Abrahams and Bauman 1971). Real, as against ideal, moral systems often accommodate more disreputability than anthropologists give them credit for, and the association between performance and disreputability has often been remarked (see Abrahams and Bauman in press). Another case that underscores the complexity of the relationship between ethics and esthetics is that of the seventeenth-century Quakers, for whom fundamental moral principles against putting oneself forward, speaking things that were in a strict sense "not the truth," and gratifying the earthly man severely limited the potential and actual domain of artistic verbal performance, leaving but a few very special kinds of outlets for performance at all (Bauman 1970, 1974, 1975). The whole matter of the relationship between ethics and esthetics is one that badly needs investigation from an anthropological point of view.

Also basic to the structure of performance events are the participants, performer(s) and audience. Performance roles constitute a major dimension of the patterning of performance within communities. As with events, certain roles will incorporate performance as a definitive attribute. Performance is necessary to establish oneself in the role, such that one cannot be considered an incumbent of the role without being a performer of verbal art, like the *sgealai,* the traditional Irish storyteller (Delargy 1945). Other roles may be more loosely associated with performance, such that members of the community have a certain expectation of performance from a person in a particular role, but it is neither required of everyone in the role nor surprising when it does not occur. Salesmen may serve as an example here, in that there is a loose expectation in contemporary American culture that salesmen are often good performers of jokes, but no one requires or expects this skill on the part of all salesmen. And, as above, other roles will have nothing to do with performance, either as definitive criterion or optional attribute.

Eligibility for and recruitment to performance roles vary cross-culturally in interesting ways. One dimension along which this variation occurs has to do with conceptions of the nature of the competence required of a performer and the way such competence is acquired (Abrahams 1972b, 1972c, reprinted in this volume; Foster 1974a:30-32; Lord 1960:21-26). Does it, for example, require special aptitude, talent, or training? Among the Limba, storytelling is a form of performance, but it is not considered to require the special talent called for in drumming and dancing. Anyone is a potential storyteller, and it calls for no special training to become one (Finnegan 1967:69-70). By contrast, the Japanese storytellers who perform *rakugo* or *kodan* must undergo a long and arduous period of training and apprenticeship before they are considered ready to practice their art (Hrdličková 1969).

Access to performance roles may have to do with other social factors relating to speaking. Among the Ashanti, artistic verbal performance is substantially the province of men, but this eligibility for performance is not without its costs. The correctness and appropriateness of women's speech in Ashanti is accepted at face value, as natural. Ashanti men, on the other hand, are under constant social pressure to prove themselves, to demonstrate their competence; this pressure extends to speaking, thus increasing the impulse toward performance (Hogan n.d.:159-65). Just as sex roles influence eligibility for performance among the Ashanti (cf. Keenan 1974), social rank plays a part in the Wolof system described by Irvine. Informants reported that the king, at the pinnacle of the nobility, must make mistakes in minor points of grammar, for correctness would imply a concern for fluency of performance, or on performance for its own sake, that is not appropriate to people of this rank (Irvine 1975).

Also to be taken into account in the analysis of performance roles is the relationship, both social and behavioral, between such roles and other roles played by the same individual. We have in mind here the way and extent to which the role of performer and the behavior associated with it may dominate or be subordinate to the other roles he may play. To illustrate one extreme possibility, we may cite Keil's assertion that in Afro-American society the role of bluesman assimilates or overshadows all other roles an adult male may normally be expected to fulfill (Keil 1966:143, 153-55). Sammy Davis, Jr. tellingly reveals the encompassing power of his role as entertainer in his statement that, "as soon as I go out the front door of my house in the morning, I'm on, Daddy, I'm on" (quoted in Messinger *et al.* 1962:98-99).

The foregoing list of patterning factors for performance has been presented schematically, for analytical and presentational convenience, but it should not be taken as a mere checklist. It should be self-evident that performance genres, acts, events, and roles cannot occur in isolation, but are mutually interactive and interdependent. Any of the above factors may be used as a point of departure or point of entry into the description and analysis of the performance system of a community, but the ultimate ethnographic statement one makes about performance as part of social life must incorporate them all in some degree. It will be useful to consider one extended example here, drawn from Joel Sherzer's description of three major ceremonial traditions of the San Blas Cuna, to give some indication how the organizing features of a performance system fit together in empirical terms (Sherzer 1974, see also Sherzer this volume).

Abstracting from Sherzer's rich description of the three traditions, we may note that each is associated with a type of event, within which specific functionaries perform particular genres in a characteristic performance mode. Thus, in the type of congress known as *omekan pela* (the women and everybody) the chiefs (*sakla*) chant (*namakke*) long chants called *pap ikar*. The chants, in turn, are interpreted to the assembled participants in the congress house by special spokesmen (*arkar*), whose speaking (*sunmakke*) also involves performance, though different from that of the chiefs. In curing rituals, a special *ikar*-knower (*ikar wisit*) speaks (*sunmakke*) the particular curing chant (each a type of *ikar*) for which he is a specialist and which is called for by the ailment from which the patient is suffering. In the third type of event, the girls' puberty ceremony, the specialist (*kantule*) in girls' puberty chants (*kantur ikar*) shouts (*kormakke*) the chants for the participants. The three performance traditions may be summarized in tabular form thus:

EVENT	ACT	ROLE	GENRE
congress (*omekan pela*)	chant (*namakke*) speak (*sunmakke*)	chief (*sakla*) spokesman (*arkar*)	chief's chant (*pap ikar*) interpretation
curing ritual	speak (*sunmakke*)	special *ikar*-knower (*ikar wisit*)	medicine chant (*kapur ikar, kurkin ikar,* etc.)
girls' puberty ceremony	shout (*kormakke*)	specialist in girls' puberty chant (*kantule*)	girls' puberty chant (*kantur ikar*)

For each ceremony or ritual to count as a valid instance of its class, the appropriate form must be rendered in the appropriate way by the appropriate functionary. That *namakke,* the *sunmakke* of the *arkar*'s interpretation and the *sunmakke* of the medicine chants, and *kormakke* all represent ways of performing for the Cuna is clear from Sherzer's description. All four roles, *sakla, arkar, ikar wisit,* and *kantule* are defined in essential part in terms of competence in these specific ways of performing their respective genres. There is thus, in these ceremonial traditions, a close and integral relationship between performance and specific events, acts, roles, and genres, and the configuration created by the interrelationships among these factors must be close to the center of an ethnography of performance among the Cuna.

Constellations such as Sherzer describes, involving events, acts, genres, and roles in highly structured and predictable combinations, constitute the nucleus of an ethnography of performance among the Cuna and are aptly made the focus of Sherzer's paper. However, it is crucial to establish that not all performance related to the system Sherzer describes is captured within the framework of conventional interrelationships outlined above. We have noted, for example, that the performance of curing *ikar* by the *ikar wisit* has its conventional locus in the curing ritual; such performance is obligatory for the *ikar wisit* to fulfill the demands of his role and for the curing ritual to be conducted at all. Against this background, then, it is noteworthy that the *ikar wisit* may also be asked to perform his *ikar* during a chicha festival associated with the girls' puberty rites, purely for entertainment. That is, the performance that has its primary place in a particular context, in which it is obligatory, may be an optional feature of another kind of event, extended to the latter because of the esthetic enjoyment to be derived from it. The association between performer and genre is maintained, but the context, and of course the function, are different.

Though optional, the performance of curing *ikar* at puberty rite festivities is no less institutionalized than the obligatory performance of these chants in curing rituals. There is no surprise or novelty in the performance of curing *ikar* at the chicha festivals. Beyond the institutionalized system, however, lies one of the most important outlets for creative vitality within the performance domain. Consider the following circumstance, involving a group of small girls whom Sherzer was using as linguistic informants. On one occasion, knowing that he was interested in the performance forms of the community, the little girls launched spontaneously into a rendition of an *arkar*'s performance as they were being recorded (Sherzer, personal communication). The remarkableness of this is apparent when one considers that the role of *arkar* is restricted to adult men, and performances of the kind the girls imitated belonged, in conventional terms, to the congress and the congress house. Though the little girls' rendition was framed as imitation, a reframing of the *arkar's* performance, it constituted performance in its own right as well, in which the girls assumed responsibility to an audience for a display of competence.

Consider one further observation made by Sherzer in his study of the Cuna. The congresses (*omekan pela*) discussed above, in which the chiefs chant their *pap ikar* and the *arkars* interpret them to the audience, are held in the congress house during the evening. During the daytime, however, when congresses are not in session, individuals who find themselves in the congress house may occasionally sit in a chief's hammock and launch into an attempt at a chief's chant, just for the fun of it (Sherzer, personal communication). Here we have what is a conventional performance doubly reframed as imitation and more importantly as play, in which there is no assumption of responsibility for a display of communicative competence, nor any assumption of responsibility for or susceptibility to evaluation for the way in which the act of expression is done.

What are the implications of these two circumstances? The little girls' performance of an *arkar's* interpretation represents a striking instance of the use of an element from the conventional, structured performance system of the community in a novel, creative, and unexpected way to fashion a new kind of performance. The playful imitation of the chief's chant involves the reframing of what is conventionally a performance genre into another mode of communication—in this case the performance genre is not performed but is rendered in another frame. Hymes (1975) applies the term "metaphrasis" to this phenomenon. In both cases, the participants are using the structured, conventional performance system itself as a resource for creative manipulation, as a base on which a range of communicative transformations can be wrought (cf. Sacks 1974). The structured system stands available to them as a set of conventional expectations and associations, but these expectations and associations are further manipulated in innovative ways, by fashioning novel performances outside the conventional system, or working various transformational adaptations which turn performance into something else. This is a very poorly documented aspect of performance systems, but one richly deserving of study, as a key to the creative vitality and flexibility of performance in a community.

5

THE EMERGENT QUALITY
OF PERFORMANCE

By stressing the creative aspect of optative performance and the normative, structured aspect of conventional performance, we do not mean to imply that the latter is fixed and frozen while creativity is confined to the former. Rather, the argument developed up to this point to highlight creativity in the use of the performance frame itself as a resource for communication provides the entrée for the final theme to be developed here—the emergent quality of all performance.[1] The concept of emergence is necessary to the study of performance as a means toward comprehending the uniqueness of particular performances within the context of performance as a generalized cultural system in a community (cf. Georges 1969:319). The ethnographic construction of the structured, conventionalized performance system standardizes and homogenizes description, but all performances are not the same, and one wants to be able to appreciate the individuality of each, as well as the community-wide patterning of the overall domain.

The emergent quality of performance resides in the interplay between communicative resources, individual competence, and the goals of the participants, within the context of particular situations. We consider as resources all those aspects of the communication system available to the members of a community for the conduct of performance. Relevant here are the keys to performance, genres, acts, events, and ground rules for the conduct of performance that make up the structured system of conventionalized performance for the community. The goals of the participants include those that are intrinsic to performance—the display of competence, the focusing of attention on oneself as performer, the enhancement of experience—as well as the other desired ends toward which performance is brought to bear; these latter will be highly culture- and situation-specific. Relative competence, finally, has to do with relative degrees of proficiency in the conduct of performance.

One of the first works to conceptualize oral literature in terms of emergent structures was Albert Lord's influential book, *The Singer of Tales* (1960), a study of Serbo-Croatian oral epic poetry for the light it sheds on the classic Homeric epic. Consider the following passage:

> Whether the performance takes place at home, in the coffee house, in the courtyard, or in the halls of a noble, the essential element of the occasion of singing that influences the form of the poetry is the variability and instability of the audience.
>
> The instability of the audience requires a marked degree of concentration on the part of the singer in order that he may sing at all; it also tests to the utmost his dramatic ability and his narrative skill in keeping the audience as attentive as possible. But it is the length of a song which is most affected by the audience's restlessness. The singer begins to tell his tale. If he is fortunate, he may find it possible to sing until he is tired without interruption from the audience. After a rest he will continue, if his audience still wishes. This may last until he finishes the song, and if his listeners are propitious and his mood heightened by their interest, he may lengthen his tale, savoring each descriptive passage. It is more likely that, instead of having this ideal occasion the singer will realize shortly after beginning that his audience is not receptive, and hence he will shorten his song so that it may be finished within the limit of time for which he feels the audience may be counted on. Or, if he

misjudges, he may simply never finish the song. Leaving out of
consideration for the moment the question of the talent of the singer,
one can say that the length of the song depends upon the audience.
(Lord 1960:16-17)

The characteristic context for the performance of the
oral epics that Lord describes is one in which the singer
competes for the attention of his audience with other factors
that may engage them, and in which the time available for
performance is of variable duration. The epic form is
remarkably well suited to the singer's combined need for
fluency and flexibility. The songs are made up of ten-syllable
end-stopped lines with a medial caesura after the fourth
syllable. In attaining competence, the singer must master a
personal stock of line and half-line formulas for expressing
character, action, and place; develop the capacity to generate
formulaic expressions on the model of his fixed formulas; and
learn to string together his lines in the development of the
narrative themes out of which his epic songs are built. The
ready-madeness of the formulas makes possible the fluency
required under performance conditions, while the flexibility of
the form allows the singer to adapt his performance to the
situation and the audience, making it longer and more
elaborate, or shorter and less adorned, as audience response,
his own mood, and time constraints may dictate. And of
course, the poetic skill of the singer is a factor in how strongly
he can attract and hold the attention of the audience, how
sensitively he can adapt to their mood, and how elaborate he
can make his song if conditions allow. Lord recorded sung
versions of the same narratives from the same singer and from
different singers that varied in length by as much as several
thousand lines.

Ultimately, one of Lord's chief contributions is to
demonstrate the unique and emergent quality of the oral text,
composed in performance. His analysis of the dynamics of the
tradition sets forth what amounts to a generative model of
epic performance. Although it has been argued that perhaps all
verbal art is generated anew in the act of performance
(Maranda 1972), there is also ample evidence to show that rote

memorization and insistence on word for word fidelity to a fixed traditional text do play a part in the performance system of certain communities (see, e.g., Friedman 1961). The point is that completely novel and completely fixed texts represent the poles of an ideal continuum, and that between the poles lies the range of emergent text structures to be found in empirical performance. The study of the factors contributing to the emergent quality of the oral literary text promises to bring about a major reconceptualization of the nature of the text, freeing it from the apparent fixity it assumes when abstracted from performance and placed on the written page, and placing it within an analytical context which focuses on the very source of the empirical relationship between art and society (cf. Georges 1969:324).

Other aspects of emergent structure are highlighted in Elinor Keenan's ethnography of the Malagasy marriage *kabary*,[2] an artful oratorical negotiation surrounding a marriage request (Keenan 1973). The *kabary* is conducted by two speechmakers, one representing the boy's family and one the girl's. The boy's speaker initiates each step of the *kabary*, which is then evaluated by the speaker for the girl. The latter may indicate that he agrees with and approves of that step, urging his opposite number on to the next, or he may state that the other's words are not according to tradition, that he has made an error in the *kabary*. The boy's speaker must then be able to justify what he has said, to show that no error has been made, or, if he admits error, he must correct it by repeating the step the right way and paying a small fine to the girl's family.

Keenan discovered, however, that there is no one unified concept of what constitutes a correct *kabary* shared by all members of the community. Rather, there are regional, familial, generational, individual, and other differences of conception and style. This being so, how is it decided what constitutes an error? There is, first of all, a preliminary meeting between the families, often with their respective speechmakers present, to establish the ground rules for the *kabary*. These are never fully conclusive, however, and it is a prominent feature of the *kabary* that arguments concerning the ground rules occur throughout the event, with appeals to the preliminary negotiations becoming simply one set of the range of possible appeals to establish authoritative performance.

Much of the impetus toward argument derives from conflicting pressures on the boy's speechmaker, who is obliged to admit to a certain range of errors, out of courtesy to the girl's family, but who is at the same time actuated by the motives of a good performance, i.e., to establish his virtuosity as a performer. The girl's speechmaker, desirous of representing the family to best advantage, is likewise concerned to display his own skill as speechmaker.

The arguments, as noted, concern the ground rules for the *kabary,* with each party insisting on the obligatory character of particular rules and features by appeal to various standards, drawn from pre-*kabary* negotiation, generational, regional, and other stylistic differences. Of particular interest is the fact that the strength of the participants' insistence on the rightness of their own way, their structural rigidity, is a function of the mood of the encounter, increasing as the tension mounts, decreasing as a settlement is approached. Ultimately, however, the practical goal of establishing an alliance between the two families involved takes precedence over all the speechmakers' insistence upon the conventions of *kabary* performance and their desire to display their performance skills; if the *kabary* threatens the making of the alliance, many are willing to reject the rules entirely to accomplish the larger goal.

The most striking feature of the marriage request *kabary* as described by Keenan is the emergent structure of the performance event itself. The ground rules for performance, as negotiated and asserted by the participants, shift and fluctuate in terms of what they bring to the event and the way it proceeds once under way. This is an extreme case, in which the competitive dimension and conflicting pressures make for an especially variable and shifting event structure, but here again the question is one of degree rather than kind, for all but the most ideally stereotyped of performance events will have discernibly variable features of act sequence and/or ground rules for performance. The emergent structure of performance events is of special interest under conditions of change, as participants adapt established patterns of performance to new circumstances. Regna Darnell provides an especially illuminating analysis of adaptation of this kind in her account of a storytelling performance by an elderly Cree informant (Darnell 1974). Called upon to tell a traditional story in a situation unlike any he could have experienced before or anticipated, the old man was able to use his competence creatively to carry off a performance. Darnell's sensitive analysis illuminates the emergent structures of both text and event.

In addition to text and event structure, we may uncover a third kind of structure emergent in performance, namely, social structure. To be sure, the emergent quality of social structure is not specific to situations involving performance. Indeed, there is an important line of inquiry in contemporary sociology which concerns itself with the creation of social structures in the course of and through all social interaction.

The principle addressed here is related to Raymond Firth's articulation, some years ago, of the distinction between social structure and social organization, in which the former is an abstract conception of ideal patterns of group relations, of conventional expectations and arrangements, and the latter has to do with "the systematic ordering of social relations by acts of choice and decision" in concrete activity. In Firth's terms, social organization is the domain of "variation from what has happened in apparently similar circumstances in the past. . . . Structural forms set a precedent and provide a limitation to the range of alternatives possible . . . but it is the possibility of alternatives that makes for variability. A person chooses, consciously or unconsciously, which course he will follow" (Firth 1961:40).

What is missing from Firth's formulation is the centrality of situated social interaction as the context in which social organization, as an emergent, takes form. The current focus on the emergence of social structures in social interaction is principally the contribution of ethnomethodology, the work of Garfinkel, Cicourel, Sacks, and others. For these sociologists, "the field of sociological analysis is anywhere the sociologist can obtain access and can examine the way the 'social structure' is a meaningful ongoing accomplishment of members" (Phillipson 1972:162). To these scholars too is owed, in large part, the recognition that language is a basic means through which social realities are intersubjectively constituted and communicated (Phillipson 1972:140). From this perspective, insofar as performance is conceived of as communicative interaction, one would expect aspects of the social structure of the interaction to be emergent from the interaction itself, as in any other such situation. Rosaldo's explication of the strategic role-taking and role-making she observed in the course of a meeting to settle a dispute over bride-price among the Ilongot illuminates the emergent aspect of social structure in that event quite clearly (Rosaldo 1973). The conventions of such meetings and the oratorical performances of the interactants endow the interaction with a special degree of formalization and intensity, but the fact that artistic verbal performance is involved is not functionally related to the negotiation of social structure on the level Rosaldo is concerned with, which has to do with such matters as the rhetorical strategies and consequences of taking the role of father in a particular event to place your interlocutor in the role of son, with its attendant obligations.

There is, however, a distinctive potential in performance by its very nature which has implications for the creation of social structure in performance. It is part of the essence of performance that it offers to the participants a special enhancement of experience, bringing with it a heightened intensity of communicative interaction which binds the audience to the performer in a way that is specific to performance as a mode of communication. Through his performance, the performer elicits the participative attention and energy of his audience, and to the extent that they value his performance, they will allow themselves to be caught up in it. When this happens, the performer gains a measure of prestige and control over the audience—prestige because of the demonstrated competence he has displayed, control because the determination of the flow of the interaction is in his hands. This general rhetorical power of performance and its potential for social control has been widely documented (Abrahams 1968; Black 1967). When the performer gains control in this way, the potential for transformation of the social structure may become available to him as well (Burke 1969 [1950] :58-59). The process is manifest in the following passage from Dick Gregory's autobiography:

> I got picked on a lot around the neighborhood. . . . I guess that's when I first began to learn about humor, the power of a joke. . . .
>
> At first . . . I'd just get mad and run home and cry when the kids started. And then, I don't know just when, I started to figure it out. They were going to laugh anyway, but if I made the jokes they'd laugh *with* me instead of at me. I'd get the kids off my back, on my side. So I'd come off that porch talking about myself. . . .
>
> Before they could get going, I'd knock it out first, fast, knock out those jokes so they wouldn't have time to set and climb all over me. . . . And they started to come over and listen to me, they'd see me coming and crowd around me on the corner. . . .
>
> Everything began to change then. . . . The kids began to expect to hear funny things from me, and after a while I could say anything I wanted. I got a reputation as a funny man. And then I started to turn the jokes on them. (Gregory 1964:54-55, italics in the original)

Through performance, Gregory is able to take control of the situation, creating a social structure with himself at the center. His first performances are ones in which he takes control by the artful use of the deprecatory humor that the other boys had formerly directed at him. The joking is still at his own expense, but he has transformed the situation, through performance, into one in which he gains admiration for his performance skills. Then, building on the control he gains through performance, he is able, by strategic use of his performance skills, to transform the situation still further, turning the humor aggressively against those who had earlier victimized him in a manner related to and reminiscent of verbal dueling (cf. Abrahams 1970b:44-58, Labov 1972b, Mitchell-Kernan 1971). In a very real sense, Gregory emerges from the performance encounters in a different social position vis-à-vis the other boys from the one he occupied before he began to perform, and the change is a consequence of his performance in those encounters.

The consideration of the power inherent in performance to transform social structures opens the way to a range of additional considerations concerning the role of the performer in society. Perhaps there is a key here to the persistently documented tendency for performers to be both admired and feared—admired for their artistic skill and power and for the enhancement of experience they provide, feared because of the potential they represent for subverting and transforming the status quo. Here too may lie a reason for the equally persistent association between performers and marginality or deviance, for in the special emergent quality of performance the capacity for change may be highlighted and made manifest to the community (see, e.g., Abrahams and Bauman 1971 and in press, Azadovskii 1926:23-25, Glassie 1971:42-52, Szwed 1971:157-65). If change is conceived of in opposition to the conventionality of the community at large, then it is only appropriate that the agents of that change be placed away from the center of that conventionality, on the margins of society.

6

CONCLUSION

The discipline of folklore (and to an extent, anthropology as well), has tended throughout its history to define itself in terms of a principal focus on the traditional remnants of earlier periods, still to be found in those sectors of society that have been outdistanced by the dominant culture. To this extent, folklore has been largely the study of what Raymond Williams has recently termed "residual culture," those "experiences, meanings and values which cannot be verified or cannot be expressed in terms of the dominant culture, [but] are nevertheless lived and practiced on the basis of the residue—cultural as well as social—of some previous social formation" (Williams 1973:10-11). If the subject matter of the discipline is restricted to the residue of a specific cultural or historical period, then folklore anticipates its own demise, for when the traditions are fully gone, the discipline loses its raison d'être (cf. Hymes 1962:678, Ben-Amos 1972:14). This need not be the case, however, for as Williams defines the concept, cultural elements may become part of residual culture as part of a continual social process, and parts of residual culture may be incorporated into the dominant culture in a complementary process. At best, though, folklore as the discipline of residual culture looks backward to the past for its frame of reference, disqualifying itself from the study of the creations of contemporary culture until they too may become residual.

Contrasted with residual culture in Williams' provocative formulation is "emergent culture," in which "new meanings and values, new practices, new significances and experiences are continually being created" (Williams 1973:11). This is a further extension of the concept of emergence, as employed in the preceding pages of this essay, but interestingly compatible with it, for the emergent quality of experience is a vital factor in the generation of emergent culture. Emergent culture, though a basic element in human social life, has always lain outside the charter of folklore, perhaps in part for lack of a unified point of departure or frame of reference able to comprehend residual forms and items, contemporary practice, and emergent structures. Performance, I would offer, constitutes just such a point of departure, the nexus of tradition, practice, and emergence in verbal art. Performance may thus be the cornerstone of a new folkloristics, liberated from its backward-facing perspective and able to comprehend much more of the totality of human experience.

NOTES

Chapter 1

1. Particularly important for folklorists is the seminal essay by Jansen (1957), and Lomax 1968, Abrahams 1968 and 1972a. Two collections which reflect the performance orientation are Paredes and Bauman 1972 and Ben-Amos and Goldstein 1975. Bauman and Sherzer 1974 reflects a wider performance orientation, of which performance in verbal art is one aspect. Singer 1958a, 1958b, and 1972 represent the perspective of an anthropologist on "cultural performances." Colby and Peacock 1973 contains a section on performance analysis, but it ignores the work of folklorists in this field, an omission which is perhaps to be expected in an article on narrative which announces its deliberate neglect of folklore journals.

2. The term "spoken art" was suggested by Thomas Sebeok in a discussion of Bascom's ideas on verbal art (Bascom 1955:246 n. 9). See also Berry 1961, Dorson 1972:9.

Chapter 2

1. Richard Ohmann, in two recent articles, employs the same passages from Austin as a point of departure for the formulation of a theory of literature based on Austin's theory of speech acts (Ohmann 1971, 1972). Ohmann's argument is interesting in places, but its productiveness is severely limited by his failure—like

Austin's—to recognize that the notion of strictly referential, "literal" meaning has little, if any, relevance to the use of spoken language in social life. For a strong critique of the concept of "ordinary language," and the impoverishing effect it has on definitions of literature, see Fish 1973.

2. The notion of frame, though not necessarily the term, is used in a similar manner by other writers: see, e.g., Huizinga 1955, Milner 1955:86, Smith 1968, Uspensky 1972, Fish 1973:52-53, Cone 1968.

3. Concerning the ecological model of communication underlying this formulation, see Sherzer and Bauman 1972 and Bauman and Sherzer 1974, 1975.

4. Note that it is *susceptibility* to evaluation that is indicated here; in this formulation the status of an utterance as performance is independent of *how* it is evaluated, whether it is judged good or bad, beautiful or ugly, etc. A bad performance is nonetheless a performance. On this point, see Hymes 1973:189-90, Mitchell-Kernan 1971:119-20.

5. I have been influenced in this formulation by Hymes 1974, Hymes 1975, d'Azevedo 1958:706, Mukařovský 1964:19, Mukařovský 1970:21, and Goffman 1974. A similar conception of performance is developed in an unfinished paper by my former colleague Joseph Doherty (Doherty MS.), whose recent tragic and untimely death occurred before he was able to complete his work. Elli Köngäs Maranda seems to be operating in terms of a conception of verbal art which is similar in certain central respects to the one developed here (Maranda 1976). Compare also Fish's conception of literature (Fish 1973). Gross's excellent article on "Art as the Communication of Competence" (Gross 1973) came to my attention after this essay was written but is congruent with it in a number of ways.

A special word should be said of the use of "competence" and "performance" in the above formulation. Use of these terms, especially in such close juxtaposition, demands at least some acknowledgment of Noam Chomsky's contribution of both to the technical vocabulary of linguistics (Chomsky 1965:3-4). It should be apparent, however, that both terms are employed in a very different way in the present work—competence in the sense advanced by Hymes (1971) and performance as formulated on page 11, above.

6. The aspect of conventionality will be discussed below.

Chapter 4

1. For other approaches to the nature and analysis of speech events, see Bauman and Sherzer 1975 and the references therein.

Chapter 5

1. The concept of emergence is developed in McHugh 1968. The emergent quality of performance is emphasized in Hymes 1975.

2. *Kabary* designates both a way of speaking and the forms in which it is manifested.

REFERENCES CITED

Abrahams, Roger D.
    1968   Introductory Remarks to a Rhetorical Theory of Folklore. Journal
                of American Folklore 81:143-148.
    1970a   A Performance-Centered Approach to Gossip. Man 5:290-301.
    1970b   Deep Down in the Jungle. Chicago: Aldine.
    1972a   Folklore and Literature as Performance. Journal of the Folklore
                Institute 8:75-94.
    1972b   Joking: The Training of the Man of Words in Talking Broad. *In*
                Rappin' and Stylin' Out. Thomas Kochman, Ed. Urbana:
                University of Illinois.
    1972c   The Training of the Man of Words in Talking Sweet. Language in
                Society: 1:15-29.
Abrahams, Roger D. and Bauman, Richard
    1971   Sense and Nonsense in St. Vincent. American Anthropologist
                73:762-772.
    in press   Ranges of Festival Behavior. *In* The Reversible World: Essays in
                Symbolic Inversion. Barbara Babcock-Abrahams, Ed. Ithaca, New
                York: Cornell University Press.
Austerlitz, Robert
    1960   Parallelismus. *In* Poetics. The Hague: Mouton.

Austin, J. L.
 1962 How to Do Things with Words. New York: Oxford University Press.

Azadovskii, Mark
 1926 Eine Sibirische Märchenerzählerin. Helsinki: Folklore Fellows Communication No. 68. English translation by James R. Dow. Austin, Texas: Center for Intercultural Studies in Folklore and Ethnomusicology.

Bascom, William
 1955 Verbal Art. Journal of American Folklore 68:245-252.

Basso, Keith
 1976 'Wise Words' of the Western Apache: Metaphor and Semantic Theory. *In* Meaning and Anthropology. Keith Basso and Henry Selby, Eds. Albuquerque: University of New Mexico.

Bateson, Gregory
 1972 Steps to an Ecology of Mind. New York: Ballantine.

Bauman, Richard
 1970 Aspects of Seventeenth-Century Quaker Rhetoric. Quarterly Journal of Speech 56:67-74.
 1972 The La Have Island General Store: Sociability and Verbal Art in a Nova Scotia Community. Journal of American Folklore 85:330-343.
 1974 Speaking in the Light: the Role of the Quaker Minister. *In* Bauman and Sherzer 1974.
 1975 Quaker Folk Linguistics and Folklore. *In* Ben-Amos and Goldstein 1975.

Bauman, Richard and Sherzer, Joel
 1974 Explorations in the Ethnography of Speaking. New York: Cambridge University Press.
 1975 The Ethnography of Speaking. *In* Annual Review of Anthropology. Volume 4. Bernard J. Siegel, Ed. Palo Alto: Annual Reviews.

Ben-Amos, Dan
 1969 Analytical Categories and Ethnic Genres. Genre 2:275-301.
 1972 Toward a Definition of Folklore in Context. *In* Paredes and Bauman 1972.

Ben-Amos, Dan and Goldstein, Kenneth (Eds.)
 1975 Folklore: Performance and Communication. The Hague: Mouton.

Berry, Jack
 1961 Spoken Art in West Africa. London: School of Oriental and African Studies, University of London.

Black, Robert
 1967 Hopi Rabbit-Hunt Chants. *In* Essays on the Verbal and Visual Arts. June Helm, Ed. Seattle: American Ethnological Society.

Bricker, Victoria R.
 1974 The Ethnographic Context of Some Traditional Mayan Speech Genres. *In* Bauman and Sherzer 1974.

Burke, Kenneth
 1969 A Rhetoric of Motives. Berkeley and Los Angeles: University of California Press.

Burns, Elizabeth
    1972   Theatricality. New York: Harper.

Chomsky, Noam
    1965   Aspects of the Theory of Syntax. Cambridge, Massachusetts: Massachusetts Institute of Technology Press.

Colby, Benjamin and Peacock, James
    1973   Narrative. *In* Handbook of Social and Cultural Anthropology. John J. Honigmann, Ed. Chicago: Rand, McNally.

Cone, Edward T.
    1968   Musical Form and Musical Performance. New York: Norton.

Crowley, Daniel J.
    1966   I Could Talk Old-Story Good: Creativity in Bahamian Folklore. Berkeley and Los Angeles: University of California Press.

Darnell, Regna
    1974   Correlates of Cree Narrative Performance. *In* Bauman and Sherzer 1974.

d'Azevedo, Warren
    1958   A Structural Approach to Esthetics: Toward a Definition of Art in Anthropology. American Anthropologist 60:702-714.

Delargy, James H.
    1945   The Gaelic Story-Teller. London: Proceedings of the British Academy.

Devereux, George
    1949   Mohave Voice and Speech Mannerisms. Word 5:268-272.

Doherty, Joseph
    MS.   Towards a Poetics of Performance.

Dorson, Richard M.
    1972   American Folklore. New York: Doubleday Anchor.

Dundes, Alan
    1966   Metafolklore and Oral Literary Criticism. The Monist 50:505-516.

Durbin, Mridula
    1971   Transformational Models Applied to Musical Analysis: Theoretical Possibilities. Ethnomusicology 15:353-362.

Enkvist, Nils E.
    1973   Linguistic Stylistics. The Hague: Mouton.

Fernandez, James
    1974   The Mission of Metaphor in Expressive Culture. Current Anthropology 15:119-145.

Finnegan, Ruth
    1967   Limba Stories and Storytelling. Oxford: Oxford University Press.
    1970   Oral Literature in Africa. Oxford: Oxford University Press.

Firth, Raymond
    1961   Elements of Social Organization. Third edition. Boston: Beacon Press paperback, 1963.

Fish, Stanley E.
    1973   How Ordinary Is Ordinary Language? New Literary History 5:40-54.

Fónagy, Ivan
    1965   Form and Function of Poetic Language. Diogenes 51:72-110.

Foster, Michael K.

1974a   From the Earth to Beyond the Sky: An Ethnographic Approach to Four Longhouse Iroquois Speech Events. Ottawa: National Museum of Man.

1974b   When Words Become Deeds: An Analysis of Three Iroquois Longhouse Speech Events. *In* Bauman and Sherzer 1974.

Fox, James

1974   Our Ancestors Spoke in Pairs. *In* Bauman and Sherzer 1974.

Frake, Charles

1964   A Structural Description of Subanun 'Religious Behavior.' *In* Explorations in Cultural Anthropology. Ward H. Goodenough, Ed. New York: McGraw-Hill.

Friedman, Albert

1961   The Formulaic Improvisation Theory of Ballad Tradition—A Counterstatement. Journal of American Folklore 74:113-115.

Georges, Robert

1969   Toward an Understanding of Storytelling Events. Journal of American Folklore 82:313-328.

Glassie, Henry

1971   Take That Night Train to Selma: An Excursion to the Outskirts of Scholarship. *In* Folksongs and Their Makers. By Henry Glassie, Edward D. Ives and John F. Szwed. Bowling Green, Ohio: Bowling Green Popular Press.

Goffman, Erving

1974   Frame Analysis: An Essay on the Organization of Experience. New York: Harper Colophon.

Gossen, Gary

1972   Chamula Genres of Verbal Behavior. *In* Paredes and Bauman 1972.

1974a   To Speak with a Heated Heart: Chamula Canons of Style and Good Performance. *In* Bauman and Sherzer 1974.

1974b   Chamulas in the World of the Sun: Time and Space in a Maya Oral Tradition. Cambridge, Massachusetts: Harvard University Press.

Gregory, Dick

1964   Nigger: An Autobiography. New York: Dutton.

Gross, Larry

1973   Art as the Communication of Competence. Social Science Information 12(5):115-141.

Havránek, Bohuslav

1964   The Functional Differentiation of the Standard Language. *In* A Prague School Reader on Esthetics, Literary Structure, and Style. Paul L. Garvin, Ed. Washington, D.C.: Georgetown University.

Hogan, Helen Marie

n.d.   An Ethnography of Communication Among the Ashanti. Austin: Penn-Texas Working Paper no. 1.

Hrdličková, V.

1969   Japanese Professional Storytellers. Genre 2:179-210.

Huizinga, Johan

1955   Homo Ludens. Boston: Beacon.

Hymes, Dell
    1962   *Review* of Indian Tales of North America, by T. P. Coffin. American Anthropologist 64:676-679.
    1966   Two Types of Linguistic Relativity (with Examples from Amerindian Ethnography). *In* Sociolinguistics. William Bright, Ed. The Hague: Mouton.
    1967   Models of the Interaction of Language and Social Setting. Journal of Social Issues 23(2):8-28.
    1971   Competence and Performance in Linguistic Theory. *In* Language Acquisition: Models and Methods. Renira Huxley and Elisabeth Ingram, Eds. London and New York: Academic Press.
    1972   Models of the Interaction of Language and Social Life. *In* Directions in Sociolinguistics. John J. Gumperz and Dell Hymes, Eds. New York: Holt, Rinehart and Winston.
    1973   An Ethnographic Perspective. New Literary History 5:187-201.
    1974   Ways of Speaking. *In* Bauman and Sherzer 1974.
    1975   Breakthrough into Performance. *In* Ben-Amos and Goldstein 1975.

Innes, Gordon
    1974   Sunjata: Three Mandinka Versions. London: School of Oriental and African Studies, University of London.

Irvine, Judith T.
    1975   Wolof Speech Styles and Social Status. Austin: Working Paper in Sociolinguistics no. 23.

Jacobs, Melville
    1959   The Content and Style of an Oral Literature. Chicago: University of Chicago.
    1972   Areal Spread of Indian Oral Genre Features in the Northwest States. Journal of the Folklore Institute 9:10-17.

Jakobson, Roman
    1960   Linguistics and Poetics. *In* Style in Language. Thomas A. Sebeok, Ed. Cambridge, Massachusetts: Massachusetts Institute of Technology Press.
    1966   Grammatical Parallelism and Its Russian Facet. Language 42:399-429.
    1968   Poetry of Grammar and Grammar of Poetry. Lingua 21:597-609.

Jansen, William Hugh
    1957   Classifying Performance in the Study of Verbal Folklore. *In* Studies in Folklore. W. Edson Richmond, Ed. Bloomington, Indiana: Indiana University Press.

Keenan, Elinor
    1973   A Sliding Sense of Obligatoriness: The Poly-Structure of Malagasy Oratory. Language in Society 2:225-243.
    1974   Norm Makers, Norm Breakers: Uses of Speech by Men and Women in a Malagasy Community. *In* Bauman and Sherzer 1974.

Keil, Charles
    1966   Urban Blues. Chicago: University of Chicago Press.

Kirshenblatt-Gimblett, Barbara
  1974   The Concept and Varieties of Narrative Performance in East European Jewish Culture. *In* Bauman and Sherzer 1974.
Labov, William
  1972a   Language in the Inner City. Philadelphia: University of Pennsylvania.
  1972b   Rules for Ritual Insults. *In* Studies in Social Interaction. David Sudnow, Ed. New York: Free Press.
Leech, Geoffrey
  1969   A Linguistic Guide to English Poetry. London: Longmans.
Lomax, Alan
  1968   Folksong Style and Culture. Washington, D.C.: American Association for the Advancement of Science.
Lord, Albert B.
  1960   The Singer of Tales. Cambridge, Massachusetts: Harvard University Press.
McDowell, John
  1974   Some Aspects of Verbal Art in Bolivian Quechua. Folklore Annual of the University Folklore Association (The University of Texas at Austin), No. 6.
McHugh, Peter
  1968   Defining the Situation. Indianapolis, Indiana: Bobbs-Merrill.
Maranda, Elli Köngäs
  1972   Theory and Practice of Riddle Analysis. *In* Paredes and Bauman 1972.
  1976   Individual and Tradition. *In* Folk Narrative Research. Studia Fennica 20:252-261.
Messinger, Sheldon L. *et al.*
  1962   Life as Theater: Some Notes on the Dramaturgic Approach to Social Reality. Sociometry 25:98-110.
Milner, Marion
  1955   Role of Illusion in Symbol Formation. *In* New Directions in Psychoanalysis. Melanie Klein, Ed. New York: Basic Books.
Mitchell-Kernan, Claudia
  1971   Language Behavior in a Black Urban Community. Berkeley: Language-Behavior Research Laboratory Monograph 2.
Mukařovský, Jan
  1964   Standard Language and Poetic Language. *In* A Prague School Reader on Esthetics, Literary Structure and Style. Paul L. Garvin, Ed. Washington, D.C.: Georgetown University.
  1970   Aesthetic Function, Norm and Value as Social Facts. Ann Arbor, Michigan: Department of Slavic Languages and Literature, University of Michigan.
Ohmann, Richard
  1971   Speech Acts and the Definition of Literature. Philosophy and Rhetoric 4:1-19.
  1972   Speech, Literature, and the Space Between. New Literary History 4:47-63.
Paredes, Américo and Bauman, Richard (Eds.)
  1972   Toward New Perspectives in Folklore. Austin: University of Texas Press.

Parry, Milman
    1933   The Traditional Metaphor in Homer. Classical Philology 28:30-43.
Phillipson, Michael
    1972   Phenomenological Philosophy and Sociology. *In* New Directions in
            Sociological Theory. By Paul Filmer, Michael Phillipson, David
            Silverman, and David Walsh. Cambridge, Massachusetts: Massachu-
            setts Institute of Technology Press.
Reaver, J. Russell
    1972   From Reality to Fantasy: Opening-Closing Formulas in the
            Structures of American Tall Tales. Southern Folklore Quarterly
            36:369-382.
Rosaldo, Michelle Z.
    1973   I Have Nothing to Hide: The Language of Ilongot Oratory.
            Language in Society 2:193-223.
Rosenberg, Bruce
    1970   The Art of the American Folk Preacher. New York: Oxford
            University Press.
Ruesch, Jurgen and Bateson, Gregory
    1968   Communication. New York: Norton.
Sacks, Harvey
    1974   An Analysis of the Course of a Joke's Telling in Conversation. *In*
            Bauman and Sherzer 1974.
Sherzer, Dina and Sherzer, Joel
    1972   Literature in San Blas: Discovering the Cuna *Ikala*. Semiotica
            6:182-199.
Sherzer, Joel
    1974   *Namakke, Sunmakke, Koirmakke*: Three Types of Cuna Speech
            Event. *In* Bauman and Sherzer 1974.

Sherzer, Joel and Bauman, Richard
    1972   Areal Studies and Culture History: Language as a Key to the
            Historical Study of Culture Contact. Southwestern Journal of
            Anthropology 28:131-152.

Singer, Milton
    1958a   From the Guest Editor. Journal of American Folklore
            71:191-204.
    1958b   The Great Tradition in a Metropolitan Center: Madras. Journal of
            American Folklore 71:347-388.
    1972   When a Great Tradition Modernizes. New York: Praeger.

Smith, Barbara H.
    1968   Poetic Closure. Chicago: University of Chicago.

Stankiewicz, Edward
    1960   Poetic Language and Non-Poetic Language in Their Interrelation.
            In Poetics. The Hague: Mouton.

Szwed, John F.
    1971   Paul E. Hall: A Newfoundland Song-Maker and Community of
            Song. *In* Folksongs and Their Makers. By Henry Glassie, Edward
            D. Ives, and John F. Szwed. Bowling Green, Ohio: Bowling Green
            University Popular Press.

Tedlock, Dennis
  1972a On the Translation of Style in Oral Literature. *In* Paredes and Bauman 1972.
  1972b Finding the Center. New York: Dial.
Toelken, J. Barre
  1969 The 'Pretty Language' of Yellowman: Genre, Mode, and Texture in Navaho Coyote Narratives. Genre 2:211-235.
Uspensky, B. A.
  1972 Structural Isomorphism of Verbal and Visual Art. Poetics 5:5-39.
Weinreich, Uriel
  1966 On the Semantic Structure of a Language. *In* Universals of Language. Joseph Greenberg, Ed. Cambridge, Massachusetts: Massachusetts Institute of Technology Press.
Williams, Raymond
  1973 Base and Superstructure in Marxist Cultural Theory. New Left Review 82:3-16.

SUPPLEMENTARY
ESSAYS

PART II

7

THE STORY IN THE STORY:

Metanarration in Folk Narrative

Barbara A. Babcock

> *. . . There is the story of one's hero, and then, thanks to the intimate connections of things, the story of one's story itself.*
>
> *Henry James (1934:313)*

One of the striking features of modern written stories is the extent to which "the story of one's story itself" has become a privileged narrative subject. Or, as the novelist William Gass observed in a recent discussion of radical developments in modern fiction,

> There are metatheorems in mathematics and logic, ethics has its linguistic oversoul, everywhere lingos to converse about lingos are being contrived, and the case is no different in the novel . . . in which the forms of fiction serve as the material upon which further forms can be imposed. (Gass 1970:24-25)

One consequence of this development is to regard and discuss such narrative self-consciousness as a singularly modern and literate phenomenon. The other—of which this study is a part—is to focus upon and reconsider the *reflexive* or *meta*-dimension of all storytelling situations and, more generally, of all sign systems. From this perspective, narrative self-commentary and stories about stories are but one expression of that

> ... "second level" aspect of symbolicity that is characteristically human, the "reflexive" capacity to develop highly complex symbol systems *about* symbol systems, the pattern of which is indicated in Aristotle's definition of God as "thought of thought," or in Hegel's dialectics of "self-consciousness." (Burke 1968:24)

Metafolklore, then, is not a recent invention of the folk despite the recent coinage of the term. "In addition to naming the speaking folklore, people [everywhere] talk about it ... folklore forms are, in and of themselves, the subject of folklore, much the same way other aspects of culture, society, and nature are" (Ben-Amos 1974:5). The term "metafolklore" was first used by Alan Dundes in 1966 in his suggestive essay, "Metafolklore and Oral Literary Criticism," in which he urged folklorists to collect and examine "folkloristic statements about folklore" as a primary source of oral literary criticism (509). And yet, only very recently and rarely have folklorists—primarily those influenced by studies in the ethnography of communication—paid any attention to the metadimension of folk expression. I would like to continue this act of attention by examining here that type of folklore that has to do with the telling of tales and may be termed *metanarration*.

To the best of my knowledge, the specific term "metanarration" was first formulated by William O. Hendricks (1973:179) on the basis of Zellig Harris's concept of "metadiscourse" (Harris 1963:40-50) to refer more specific-ally to narrative discourse about narrative discourse.[2] As such, the concept also partakes of the notion of "metalanguage" and "second-order language" as developed by Jakobson (1960), Hjelmslev (1961), and, following the latter, by Barthes (1967).

More recently, John McDowell (1973) has similarly used the term and the concept in an analysis of an American folk sermon to describe references to the performance setting which intrude upon the narration itself (141). The term as I use it in this discussion also derives from the literary critical concepts of "metanovel" and "metafiction" as developed and discussed by Hugh Kenner (1962) and Robert Scholes (1970) respectively, and of *"metarécit"* as much discussed in French narrative scholarship, especially by Tzvetan Todorov (1967, 1971a, and 1971b), and Gérard Genette (1969, 1972).

Given the widespread concern among literary critics with the meta- or reflexive dimension of all forms of literature, one would do well to question why this aspect of folk narrative has been so little studied. One reason for this strange and unfortunate omission in folk narrative scholarship might be described, following Todorov (1971a), as "the myth of primitive narrative." This theory postulates that oral or folk narrative is simple, natural, and direct—uncontaminated by the devices, digressions, and structural complexities of the modern, written tale. Most importantly, it regards oral narrative as uncomplicated by the latter's conscious forms of self-commentary. By extention, this approach (which is characteristic of functional discussions) "implicitly insinuates the assumption that, to put it crudely, 'primitive peoples' have no idea of aesthetics" (Finnegan 1970:331). Or, at best, that they simply tell stories without any conscious articulation of the esthetic thereof.

Another assumption of the "myth of primitive narrative" is that such "other" narratives are fundamentally different from "our" literary ones and, therefore, can and should be analyzed by different criteria than those we apply to literary narrative. This dichotomy is perpetuated by the very fact that students of "folk" or "primitive" literary traditions have insisted on calling their subject by another name such as folklore or verbal art (Hymes 1973:198).[3] While oral narrative *is* different, that which makes it different—its oral quality—is often not seriously considered. The unfortunate result of this bias for folk narrative studies "has too often been to play down the literary aspect[s and esthetic qualities] or even to explain [them] away completely" (Finnegan 1970:317).[4]

A third possible reason for the ignoring or eschewing of narrative's meta-dimension is the concern of folkloristics (like other humanistic disciplines) to establish the "science of folklore." The consequence of this concern is the systematic consideration of the "objective" aspects of narratives, of the "texts" (or the separable content of narrative performances) that have been collected.[5] While this has been a productive strategy—especially in recent oral formulaic and structural analyses of separable content—for perceiving the enstructuring and dissemination and the distinctive features and the structural commonalities of a group of narratives, it has also had some considerably less positive results. One is that the majority of our collections of folk narrative consist of texts which record little more than narrative content and, all too often, only a skeletal "plot summary" of that. Such "texts" are so removed from the performance situation of the telling of the tale that it becomes difficult (if not impossible) to examine the "texture" and the "context" of the text[6] or to study any folk narrative problem other than its construction, dissemination, and "deep structure." With few exceptions we have tended to study the tale at the expense of its teller, telling, and reception. A more serious consequence is that such narrative texts devoid of contexts are often "logically satisfactory synthes[es] which would perhaps be unintelligible to most members of the indigenous culture" (Turner 1974:159).[7]

Admittedly, the tendency to translate actual narrative performance into essentially third-person, "objective" accounts has been offset somewhat by interest in such first-person narratives as *Memoräten.* But even here, the emphasis is on the past events which the story recounts and not on the personal, interactional elements of the tales as they are told—i.e., how telling a story about something that happened to one's self in the first person establishes a special kind of relationship with one's audience.

In other words, the majority of folk narrative studies have been preoccupied with that aspect of narrative which Benveniste calls *histoire,* the story of past events, at the expense of its *discours,* those aspects of narrative and narrative performance which pertain to the process of communication, the relationship between speaker and hearer, (Benveniste 1966:237-50). Or, in Roman Jakobson's terms, we have tended to focus on the "narrated event" and to neglect the "speech event" within which the former is presented (Jakobson 1957:492-93). When we base our study of narrative on the edited text (or composite texts) of the *histoire* or narrated event, we not only eliminate texture and context, we confine ourselves to a very particular mode of language "defined by a number of exclusions and restrictive conditions such as the denial of present tense, first person, etc." (Genette 1966:162). We thereby create a false and ideal narrative situation, for the narration of past events never exists without such admixture of discourse which is our "natural" mode of speaking and which inevitably frames the tale that is told. Narration is communication and "every communication has a content *and* a relationship aspect such that the latter classifies the former and is therefore a metacommunication" (Watz-lawick *et al.* 1967:54). From this perspective it is easy to see why the meta- dimension of folk narrative has been slighted: the majority of self-commenting devices belong to the *discours* rather than the *histoire.*

This text-centered approach has changed somewhat as a result of (1) the presence of the theoretical folklorist in the field as well as in the library, and (2) considerable recent interest in narrative *as performance.* In our presenting of data, we now include the dynamics of performance as enacted, the immediate context of performance, and the larger socio-cultural context. Even in our concern with context, however, we have tended to focus on *para*linguistic (gestures, laughter, applause, etc.) rather than *meta*linguistic aspects of contexts and to ignore the literary or generic context in which a narrative is placed and upon which its perception and appreciation depend.[8] With the exception of several recent studies in performance-centered approaches to folklore and in the ethnography of speaking,[9] we have little information on and analysis of the metacommunicative situating devices which every performer uses to set up "an interpretative frame within which the messages being communicated are to be understood" (Bauman this volume:9). Given the traditional interest of folklorists in texts and their new-found concern with "filling in the context," it seems ironic that those very contextualizing devices found *within* the texts themselves—verbal metacommunicative markers—may be the least recorded (and perhaps most suppressed).

Metacommunication in narrative performance may be described as any element of communication which calls attention to the speech event as a performance and to the relationship which obtains between the narrator and his audience vis-à-vis the narrative message. By focusing our attention on the act or process of communicating, such devices lead us away from and then back to the message by supplying a "frame," an interpretative context or alternative point of view within which the content of the story is to be understood and judged.[10] When, for example, the blues singer says in the middle of his song, "hear me singing to you," or the epic singer describes a scene in which an epic singer is singing and then says, "Where would these heroes be without an epic singer to sing their praises?," we are reminded that a special mode of speaking pertains and that a special person is creating this communication.

While *metacommunication* or *framing* may be used as the domain term for all such devices, both verbal and nonverbal, that categorize and comment upon the communicative event, it should also be noted that self-reference may occur not only with respect to the speech event in general, but more specifically with regard to any of the individual factors or dimensions of the speech event as defined and described in Jakobson (1960) and Hymes (1972). Within the external frame of the performance, specific reference is often made to the performer, the audience, the message, the code, the channel or medium of expression, the register, etc., or to any combination thereof. For example, the blues singer's "hear me singing to you" calls attention to the singer, the audience, and the relationship between them which is made through the channel of singing. This example also illustrates the metacommunicative importance of pronomial usage. Pronouns are "purely relational units" that encode the relationship obtaining between sender and receiver and as such may be used (as they are in this aside) to shift one's attention from the narrated event to the speech event and vice-versa (Jakobson 1968:600-603; 1957).

Since *metacommunication* refers generally to framing devices and to the relationship between speaker and hearer in *any* speech event, I would suggest that we use the term *metanarration* to refer specifically to narrative performance and discourse and to those devices which comment upon the narrator, the narrating, and the narrative both as message and as code. Metanarrative remarks, such as the following that Dundes reports from a joke and a story, not only comment on the event as a special type of performance and the relationship between the teller and the told, but refer specifically to a marked genre feature and, thus, to the generic pattern being drawn upon or played with:

> It was a dark and stormy night and this guy goes up to this old farmhouse. He's a salesman and he says to the farmer, "I'm a salesman, my car broke down, and I need a place to stay." And the farmer says, "That's all right, but there's just one thing, we have no extra rooms to spare so you'll have to sleep with my son." And the salesman says, "Oh my God, I must be in the wrong joke."

and,

> "Well there was once, there was a little boy. There was always a little boy, you know, and. . . ." (Dundes 1966:509-11)

The first is an example of a joke about a joke cycle that turns on and thereby comments on a critical content feature of the cycle: the farmer usually tells the salesman that the only available space is in his daughter's room. The second example similarly remarks upon a generic feature, a critical aspect of the narrative code. In this case, the comment indicates that there are a great many tales with little boys in them and serves to authenticate the particular joke being told. As Dundes points out, "It is as if to say that traditional tales must have little boys in them as protagonists and so in this traditional tale I am about to tell there is this required stereotyped character" (Dundes 1966:511).

Metanarration, then, may be said to combine those forms of self-commentary that Bateson distinguished as *metacommunicative* and *metalinguistic*. In a metacommunicative utterance, "the subject of discourse is the relationship between speakers (e.g., 'my telling you where to find the cat was friendly,' or 'this is play')"; in a metalinguistic comment, "the subject of discourse is the language (e.g., 'The word, cat, has no fur and cannot scratch')" (Bateson 1972 [1955]:178). Jakobson similarly defines the metalinguistic function as speech that is focused on the *code* and on the problems involved in decoding the message. Insofar as it may refer to the performance setting, the performance itself and the genre to which it belongs, and/or the performer and his audience, a metanarrational comment may refer to any of the factors constituting the speech event and may be either metacommunicative or metalinguistic or both. More specifically, metanarration usually involves a combined emphasis on what Jakobson describes as the *metalinguistic function; the phatic* function, a focusing on the medium of communication, the channel; and the *poetic* function, the "set to the message" or attention to the message for its own sake (Jakobson 1960:353-58). By this I do not mean to imply that metanarrative devices do not focus on other factors of the narrative event, but simply that the majority of such comments refer to the code, message, or channel of narrative communication. In metanarration the subject of discourse is the narrative itself and those elements by which it is constituted and communicated.

Examples such as those reported by Dundes and more recently by Ben-Amos (1974) in which the story, joke or proverb actually turns on the reference to the code are important as explicit instances of metafolklore. Most metanarrative devices, however, are not so dramatically self-evident because we are habituated to them and because they do not call attention to themselves as such. As Richard Ohmann rightly remarks, "Once upon a time" has become a ghostly presence at the beginning of all narrative (Ohmann 1972:53). Many such metanarrative comments seldom get reported (even if self-evident) because we take them for granted and because they convey very little narrative information and are not, therefore, regarded as relevant to the dramatic structure, the events of the story. How often for instance does one find in collections of jokes that most common joking device, "Have you heard this one already?" Only when it occurs in a joke such as "What has four legs, wags its tail and barks? A dog? Oh, you've heard that one already" does it seem of special note and then as an anomaly.

Essentially, to point up these meta- features is simply to relate narrative to what has been argued for all language use. One of the axioms of recent structural studies of language (stemming from Jakobson's discussions of aphasia) is that self-reference is a basic attribute of speech communication, for if we don't have a means of talking about talk we can neither learn to speak properly nor make certain that our message is getting through. Because the ability to metacommunicate appropriately is "the *condition sine qua non* of successful communication" and is "intimately linked with the enormous problem of awareness of self and other" (Watzlawick *et al.* 1967:53), various forms of pathological communication such as aphasia have been defined as the inability to metacommunicate. Thus, it is generally asserted that "every enunciation involves a kind of lateral statement about language, which is to say about itself as well, and includes a kind of self-designation within its very structure" (Jameson 1972:202). And, regarding narrative specifically, Todorov similarly asserts that "every story relates, across the plot of events, the story of its own creation, of its own story" (Todorov 1967:49). This reflexive frame, or "self-designation within its very structure" is especially important in esthetic expression, for

> a symbol would cease to be a symbol and become, in our consciousness, a simple reality in its own right, without any relation to the thing symbolized, if the description has as its object only reality: description must necessarily contain the symbolic nature of these very symbols; it must deliberately and consistently hold on to both the symbol and the thing symbolized. *The description must be double.* This duality is obtained through a critique of the symbols themselves. . . . In order to perceive the world of the work of art as a sign system it is necessary (although not always sufficient) to designate its borders; it is precisely these borders which create the representation. (Uspensky 1973:139-40)

The storyteller not only must create an illusion of reality but must make certain that we are aware that it *is* an illusion, and for this metanarration is essential.

This framing is obviously more of a problem in apparently spontaneous talk than in more highly formulaic and predictable narrative, where one would imagine that this kind of code-checking need not occur so often. Judging, however, by the strictly impressionistic data that anyone who has engaged in storytelling sessions carries around, the process is just as important. Again, the presence of code-checking devices in narrative indicates how important the folk concepts of genres are.[11] Such self-referencing asks those participating to observe how the individual item conforms or departs from the pattern of expectation common to other examples of the type. Which is not to argue that the genre/code equation is complete, nor that the performer is doing nothing more than fulfilling the expectation pattern. To the contrary, it is with just such self-designating comments that he is able to call attention both to the application of generic features and to the ways in which he, as performer, is able to manipulate these patterns, to use them for his own expressive purposes. Metadevices become even more important in those renditions in which play is added to play—that is, when genre-based expectations are drawn ultimately to be frustrated as most obviously in narrative parody (e.g., Tale 20 of the Winnebago Trickster Cycle plays upon the traditional old woman helper figure in Winnebago narrative who here assists the false heroine [trickster] in seducing the chief's sons) or in narratives such as Dundes cites that turn on a reference to the code.

To the extent that *metanarration* makes a critique of the features and performance of narrative itself, it is probably our clearest way of understanding what Dundes describes as "folk poetics"—the *-emic* system of esthetic classification and assessment. Before we impose our own literary conventions on folk narrative or assume that it has no esthetic, we would do well to look at the ways in which the tales themselves tell us both implicitly and explicitly what their conventions and standards of esthetic judgment are.

One of the most important *metanarrative* devices which has been widely reported and which we would do well to examine from this perspective is the beginning and ending or opening and closing formulae of narrative.[12] "Beginnings" and "endings" are of crucial importance in the formulation of systems of culture; in narrative they are one of the ways in which a narrator sets up an interpretative frame which tells us this is play, this is performance, or more specifically, this is such and such type of story and should be understood and judged accordingly. This marked external frame, like previously discussed examples, is an instance of *explicit* metanarration—that is, of a comment that deliberately calls attention to the narrative performance *as* performance and communication and openly refers to the definitive features of the specific genre.

This external metanarrative frame may be compounded by various means of narrative embedding: of placing tales within tales within tales. . . . The opening and closing formulae may themselves become a narrative, a "frame story" (often related in the first person) which comments upon the "real" story which is related within it as in, for example, *1001 Nights*. The frame tale, the embedding narrative is the essence of metanarration for it is the narration of a narration that calls attention to the act of narrating itself (cf. Todorov 1971b:85). Self-commentary in the form of embedding also occurs in a typical field collecting situation in which the informant tells the folklorist a story about an occasion on which he told a story and then tells that story, as Barbara Kirshenblatt-Gimblett describes in "A Parable in Context" (1975) and significantly analyzes as an example of metanarrative embedding. Another type of embedding is the authentication formula which involves telling another story. As Daniel Crowley reports, the Bahamians call this device, which plays on the word "story," a "double lie": "And the kick he pass at me, now I going tell you the truth, that kick kick me from here to the British Colonial hotel but I ain't going to tell you the damn lie, it kick me from here to your building" (1966:27). Even more explicitly, the embedded story itself may be a story about someone telling a story as are the Sinbad the Sailor tales of *1001 Nights*.[13] Then too, the frame tale may become the tale in its entirety as in innumerable narratives about the telling of stories such as the Bahamian tale Crowley recorded, "King Dislikes Repetition" (1966:139-40) or the Donegal story recorded by Séamas O Cathain of "The Man Who Had No Story" (1973). In such cases, metanarration is no longer a separable part of the narrative but is narration itself.

Not all metanarration, however, is so overt and so explicit. We need also to look at those *implicit* forms of narrative self-commentary and self-reference that constitute much of what we describe as the "texture" of the text.[14] First of all, various forms of narrative repetition (including the explicit embedding or interior duplication previously discussed) have, in addition to their forestalling and suspense-building function, the metanarrative function of pointing up the importance of perspective by presenting the same event from different points of view. In other words, repetition not only raises the repeated word(s) and its referent to a different level, "making it present," it also calls our attention to the act of "presenting." Repetitions such as the recurrent song of the *cante-fable*, the audience's repeating of a certain line, or the use of a "Number Two Man" who repeats and responds to the narrator's lines perform the phatic function of calling attention to the channel of communication and the conative one of assuring audience participation. Perhaps the most pervasive form of repetition as implicit metanarration is canonical parallelism, identified by Jakobson as a central and defining feature of much of the world's oral poetry (1960, 1966, 1968).[15]

And, then, there are innumerable devices such as naming, quoting, onomatopoeia, the use of different styles, pronoun shifts, changes in channel or media, the use of different languages or other register shifts such as the intermixture of narrative and song or prose and verse which are implicitly metanarrational. A shift in pronouns or tense implicitly comments on the story or the storytelling by effecting a transfer from an internal point of view to an external one—i.e., from the narrated event to the speech event—or vice versa. On the other hand devices such as quotations, parenthetical asides, and changes in channel or register make an implicit commentary through using language in an undetermined way, i.e., through a mixture of logical types. They are the storyteller's means of establishing an implicit dialogue with his own and other narrative texts. All such devices which move our attention from one factor of the narrative event to another, from one level of the narrative to another, from one orientation to another within a given level, or from one logical type to another are instances of metanarration in that they involve reference to the act of speech in which they are used. As such they might be properly described and analyzed following Jakobson (1957) and Weinreich (1966) as "shifters" or "deictic signs." All perform the metanarrational functions of establishing the position of the narrator and the audience vis-à-vis the story, call attention to the problems and processes of narration as an act, and provide a frame for interpretation.

On a larger scale, there are entire stories or classes of stories about various forms of artificing or making fictions which are *implicitly* metanarrational. Perhaps no form of narrative does this so fully as the ubiquitous trickster tale.

Trickster is after all, an artificer of stories (among other things); that's how he gets by, through manufacturing lies. One might want to rejoin that there is a difference between telling stories and telling lies, but this is to forget that in many cultures no such distinction is made. Thus, in a very real sense there is an alliance set up between storyteller and trickster, and the stories of the one comment on the stories of the other.[16] Between them, the group is reminded of man's protean capacities, especially when he is given license to fabricate stories other than "truthful" ones. In St. Vincent, West Indies, for example, the term for tale is *Nansi 'tory*; ostensibly referring to the spider trickster, *Anansi*; the term also draws upon the semantic fields of *nonsense* (meaning a licentious performance), *nas'y* (nasty), and *'tory* (meaning outright lie). These then are regarded by Vincentians as stories (by which they mean licensed narrative lies, closely aligned to gossip, for instance, except that they are told on a special occasion such as a wake) about a storymaker, an antisocial character who lives by his wits and by making up stories, lies. *Anansi* is regarded as *rude, vextatious,* and one who leads to *melee* (fighting)—the very same terms that are often used to describe the storytelling occasion and, by extension, the storyteller (Abrahams 1970).

If this seems like an unnatural set-up, consider our own concept of "story." *Telling a story,* at least in American standard speech, refers more often to narrating a personal event than anything else. And these personal events are often of the gossiping sort, in which the event being narrated is a story which someone told to someone else about someone else (perhaps even the storyteller). This is why personal pronouns often present such a problem in such storytelling sessions and why they merit our attention as a *metanarrative* device, as "shifters."

Finally, there is yet another class of narratives that are both implicitly and explicitly metanarrational in their concern with the relations between cosmological, social, and esthetic orders. For both an *-etic* and *-emic* understanding of these relations we would do well to examine innumerable *meta-myths* about how men got words and how they got stories—myths which often link man's revolt and separation from the gods with speaking, which describe the uses and abuses of telling stories and creation and destruction by the word.[17] As the brilliant full-length analyses of Calame-Griaule (1965) and Gossen (1972 reprinted this volume, 1974) demonstrate, metamyth, like metanarration generally, shows us how verbal art is defined and organized from the native point of view and can give us "the means of circumventing the a priori analytical definition of verbal art in favor of the esthetic principles by which the people themselves define artistic verbal performance and shape artistic structures" (Bauman and Sherzer 1974:314). If we listen, every storyteller tells us "the story of [his] story itself."

NOTES

1. The original version of this paper was presented at the 6th International Folk Narrative Congress in Helsinki, Finland, June, 1974 and published in Folk Narrative Research. Studia Fennica 20 (1976):177-184. In the original formulation as well as the revision of these ideas about metanarration I am very much indebted to several colleagues and friends: Roger D. Abrahams, Rilda Baker, Richard Bauman, Archie Green, Paul Schmidt, and Susan Wittig.

2. In using the term "metanarration" I do not mean to imply a connected text about the text, which is only rarely the case. Rather I use it to refer to any and all components of a story which function reflexively or self-critically. For this distinction cf. Hendricks 1973:191 and Harris 1963:50.

3. In "Folklore and the Structural Analysis of Literary Texts" (1970), Hendricks makes a similar argument against the attitudinal barriers which separate "folklore" from "literature."

4. For the argument that the diminished literary value of much oral literature is the consequence of our methods of collecting and translating see Tedlock 1972 and Hymes 1973.

5. This emphasis in folkloristic and anthropological studies on the story, the structure of narrated events, is undoubtedly influenced by and may well be a consequence of the once pervasive emphasis in literary studies on "showing" versus "telling."

6. See Dundes 1964 for distinctions among and discussion of these three aspects of folklore form.

7. Tedlock 1972 and Hymes 1973 similarly argue that unless we present texts in terms of the circumstances under which they were obtained we are in danger of producing "a sketch of how a story goes, but not a *doing* of the narrative."

8. For careful and detailed discussion of the *paralinguistic* features of narrative texts see Tedlock 1972.

9. See in particular Kirshenblatt-Gimblett 1975; Gossen 1972, 1974; Toelken 1969; Abrahams 1970; Paredes and Bauman 1972; Bauman and Sherzer 1974; and Bauman 1975.

10. Following Bateson, 1972 [1955] and Goffman 1974, Bauman (this volume:16) asserts that "all framing . . . is accomplished through the employment of culturally conventionalized metacommunication."

11. For discussion of genre as *an* if not *the* most important instance of metafolklore see Ben-Amos 1974:3-6.

12. See Bauman this volume:16-22 for an etic list of other devices which function like opening and closing formulae to "key" performance.

13. For further discussion and analysis of narrative embedding see Todorov's analysis of the *Decameron* 1969.

14. For brilliant and detailed discussion of implicit and internal framing in the verbal and the visual arts, see Uspensky 1973: Chapter 7.

15. For recent discussions of parallelism, see the essays by Gossen, Bricker, and Fox in Bauman and Sherzer 1974.

16. In this regard, Lévi-Strauss's insistence on and practice of explicating "mythe par mythe" is particularly interesting. Even more interesting is his repeated use of a trickster myth to mediate and to explain the initially less than obvious connections between two or more other myths.

17. Myths such as I refer to here are explicitly meta-. Lévi-Strauss (1964:346) asserts that *all* myth is meta- insofar as its implicit if not explicit subject is the emergence of language or communication. For further discussion of this type of metanarrative see my " 'In the Beginning Was the Word': Myth as Meta-," paper presented at the 1974 Annual American Folklore Society Meeting; forthcoming in the *Journal of American Folklore*.

REFERENCES CITED

Abrahams, Roger D.
    1970   A Performance-Centered Approach to Gossip. Man 5:290-301.
Barthes, Roland
    1967   Système de la Mode. Paris: Seuil.
Bateson, Gregory
    1972 [1955] A Theory of Play and Fantasy. *In* Steps to an Ecology of Mind.
                New York: Ballantine.
Bauman, Richard
    1975   Verbal Art as Performance. American Anthropologist 77:290-311.
Bauman, Richard, and Sherzer, Joel (Eds.)
    1974   Explorations in the Ethnography of Speaking. New York:
            Cambridge University Press.
Ben-Amos, Dan
    1974   Folklore in African Society. Folklore Preprint Series 2(1):1-32.
Benveniste, Emile
    1966   Problèmes de linguistique générale. Paris: Gallimard.
Burke, Kenneth
    1968   Language as Symbolic Action. Berkeley: University of California
            Press.
Calame-Griaule, Geneviève
    1965   Ethnologie et langage: La parole chez les Dogon: Paris: Gallimard.
Crowley, Daniel J.
    1966   I Could Talk Old-Story Good: Creativity in Bahamian Folklore.
            Berkeley and Los Angeles: University of California Press.
Dundes, Alan
    1964   Texture, Text, and Context. Southern Folklore Quarterly
            28:251-261.
    1966   Metafolklore and Oral Literary Criticism. The Monist 50:505-516.
Finnegan, Ruth
    1970   Oral Literature in Africa. Oxford: Oxford University Press.
Gass, William
    1970   Fiction and the Figures of Life. New York: Knopf.
Genette, Gérard
    1966   Frontières du récit. Communications 8:152-163.
    1969   Figures II. Paris: Seuil.
    1972   Figures III. Paris: Seuil.
Goffman, Erving
    1974   Frame Analysis: An Essay on the Organization of Experience.
            New York: Harper Colophon.
Gossen, Gary
    1972   Chamula Genres of Verbal Behavior. *In* Paredes and Bauman 1972.
    1974   Chamulas in the World of the Sun: Time and Space in a Maya Oral
            Tradition. Cambridge, Massachusetts: Harvard University Press.
Harris, Zellig
    1963   Discourse Analysis Reprints. The Hague: Mouton.

Hendricks, William O.
>1970   Folklore and the Structural Analysis of Literary Texts. Language and Style 3:83-121.
>1973   Methodology of Narrative Structural Analysis. Semiotica 7:167-188.

Hjelmslev, Louis
>1961   Prolegomena to a Theory of Language. Madison: University of Wisconsin Press.

Hymes, Dell
>1972   Models of the Interaction of Language and Social Life. *In* Directions in Sociolinguistics. John J. Gumperz and Dell Hymes, Eds. New York: Holt, Rinehart and Winston.
>1973   An Ethnographic Perspective. New Literary History 5:187-201.

Jakobson, Roman
>1957   Shifters, Verbal Categories, and the Russian Verb: Description and Analysis of Contemporary Standard Russian. Cambridge, Massachusetts: Massachusetts Institute of Technology Press.
>1960   Linguistics and Poetics. *In* Style in Language. Thomas A. Sebeok, Ed. Cambridge, Massachusetts: Massachusetts Institute of Technology Press.
>1966   Grammatical Parallelism and Its Russian Facet. Language 42:399-429.
>1968   Poetry of Grammar and Grammar of Poetry. Lingua 21:597-609.

James, Henry
>1934   The Art of the Novel. New York: Scribner.

Jameson, Frederick
>1972   The Prison House of Language. Princeton, New Jersey: Princeton University Press.

Kenner, Hugh
>1962   Flaubert, Joyce and Beckett: The Stoic Comedians. Boston: Beacon Press.

Kirshenblatt-Gimblett, Barbara
>1975   A Parable in Context. *In* Folklore: Performance and Communication. Dan Ben-Amos and Kenneth S. Goldstein, Eds. The Hague: Mouton.

Lévi-Strauss, Claude
>1964   Mythologiques I: Le Cru et le Cuit. Paris: Plon.

McDowell, John
>1973   Performance and the Folkloric Text: A Rhetorical Approach to 'The Christ of the Bible.' Folklore Forum 6(3):139-148.

Ó Cathain, Séamas
>1973   The Man Who Had No Story. Unpublished manuscript.

Ohmann, Richard
>1972   Speech, Literature and the Space Between. New Literary History 4:47-63.

Paredes, Américo and Bauman, Richard (Eds.)
>1972   Toward New Perspectives in Folklore. Austin: University of Texas Press.

Scholes, Robert
>1970   Metafiction. The Iowa Review 1(4):100-115.

Tedlock, Dennis
    1972   On the Translation of Style in Oral Narrative. *In* Paredes and Bauman 1972.

Todorov, Tzvetan
    1967   Littérature et signification. Paris: Librairie Larousse.
    1969   Grammaire du Décaméron. The Hague: Mouton.
    1971a   Poétique de la prose. Paris: Seuil.
    1971b   Les hommes-récits. *In* Poetique de la prose. Paris: Seuil.

Toelken, J. Barre
    1969   The 'Pretty Language' of Yellowman: Genre, Mode, and Texture in Navaho Coyote Narratives. Genre 2:211-235.

Turner, Victor W.
    1974   The Word of the Dogon. *In* Dramas, Fields, and Metaphors. Ithaca: Cornell University Press.

Uspensky, Boris
    1973   A Poetics of Composition: The Structure of the Artistic Text and Typology of a Compositional Form. Berkeley and Los Angeles: University of California.

Watzlawick, Paul, Beavin, Janet Helmick and Jackson, Don D.
    1967   Pragmatics of Human Communication: A Study of Interactional Patterns, Pathologies, and Paradoxes. New York: Norton.

Weinreich, Uriel
    1966   On the Semantic Structure of a Language. *In* Universals of Language. Joseph Greenberg, Ed. Cambridge, Massachusetts: Massachusetts Institute of Technology Press.

8

CHAMULA GENRES OF
VERBAL BEHAVIOR[1]

Gary H. Gossen

The principal purpose of this paper is to present a brief taxonomy of Chamula folk genres of verbal behavior. This will contribute some substantive data to what is becoming increasingly well known: that European genre labels are often inadequate for description of non-Western oral traditions. Secondly, I will suggest that the whole domain of Chamula verbal behavior offers more opportunities for context-conscious interpretation of the meaning of oral tradition in Chamula life than single genres considered separately. This approach constitutes an application of certain -emic methods of data collection and analysis which have been known in anthropology as ethnoscience, ethnomethodology, ethnographic semantics, and ethnography of communication. Consideration of the importance of folk genres of non-Western oral traditions has appeared only sporadically until quite recently, although folklorists and anthropologists in the past

This essay is reprinted by permission from *Toward New Perspectives in Folklore*, A. Paredes and R. Bauman, editors. Austin: Univ. of Texas Press, 1972, pp. 145-167.

decade have been giving more and more attention to native classification of genres and related behavior settings. Thirdly, although I generally agree that native taxonomies have intrinsic descriptive value, I do not think they stand alone as ends in themselves for the purpose of analysis. I wish to go beyond this to suggest that Chamula oral tradition constitutes an ethical statement whose categories (genres) are organized according to attributes which also organize other aspects of Chamula expressive behavior and values. In this way, the structure of the whole of Chamula oral tradition may be seen to be isomorphic with the structures of other aspects of Chamula life such as religion and world view.

Finally, I hope to show that a holistic approach to Chamula verbal behavior is useful for describing and analyzing linguistic aspects of the socialization process. Formal genres that relate to ritual settings presuppose knowledge of other, more informal genres, which are learned in secular settings at an earlier age. This leads to a criticism of the tendency among many folklorists and anthropologists to deal with "standard narrative genres" (particularly myth, legend, and folktale) in preference to the (apparently) less substantial "minor genres." This tendency is unfortunate, for, at least in the case of the Chamulas, the less formal narrative and nonnarrative genres are vitally important for passing on information and for regulating social relations, as well as serving as aids in recognizing, understanding, and performing the more formal genres. In fact, the Chamula data indicate that the categories of the universe are as well encoded in gossip, riddles, and proverbs as they are in myth—Claude Lévi-Strauss's statement that myth has "special meaning" notwithstanding (Lévi-Strauss 1963).

The Community

Chamula is a Tzotzil-speaking *municipio* of approximately 40,000 Maya Indians, lying at the top of the Chiapas Highlands of southern Mexico. Average elevation is about 7,600 feet. All Chamulas engage to a greater or lesser extent in swidden agriculture, the subsistence base consisting of maize, beans, squash, and cabbage in approximately that order of importance. Nearly all Chamula families also keep a few sheep for wool production, for their own clothing and for a small surplus sold to Indians in nearby *municipios*. They also keep chickens, turkeys, and, occasionally, rabbits. In the many cases in which their own land is insufficient to produce enough food, Chamulas engage in economic specializations—such as the manufacture of charcoal, pottery, sandals, and furniture— or seek employment as day laborers. Sources of this wage labor are San Cristóbal, the principal Spanish-speaking trade center in the region, and the Pacific Lowlands, where they work either on Ladino-owned coffee plantations or in cornfields rented by the neighboring Zinacanteco Indians, who also speak Tzotzil. Tzotzil belongs to the Tzeltalan group (Tzotzil, Tzeltal and Tojolabal) of Maya languages. Tzotzil is spoken by approximately 100,000 persons in the state of Chiapas. Chamula is one of nine predominantly Indian *municipios* where it is spoken. Each of these communities has a separate dialect, costume, and set of customs.

Chamulas live patrilocally in over one hundred dispersed hamlets belonging to one or more of the three *barrios* of the *municipio*. The three *barrios* converge on a ceremonial center that has virtually no permanent population. Rental houses there provide temporary homes for the political and religious officials while they serve their terms in office, ranging from one to three years. They then return to their outlying hamlets. Chamulas are governed by a political hierarchy, partly traditional (Ayuntamiento Regional, consisting of sixty-two positions or *cargos*) and partly prescribed by Mexican law (Ayuntamiento Constitucional, consisting of six positions, including that of the chief magistrate, the *presidente*). A religious hierarchy consisting of sixty-one major positions supervises ceremonial activities and cults to the saints and also coordinates its ritual activities with those of the political hierarchy. Political authority on the local level lies in the hands of past *cargo* holders and heads of segments of patrilineages. Religious authority in the hamlets is exercised by shamans, past holders of religious *cargos,* and heads of segments of patrilineages.

Chamula religion and cosmology form a complex syncretistic system, which is the product of sixteenth-century Spanish Catholicism and pre-Columbian Maya cults to nature deities, particularly to the sun (now identified with Christ), the moon (now the same as the Virgin Mary), water spirits, and earth lords. The other saints, including the patron saint of Chamula, San Juan, are kinsmen of the sun. The sun is the son of the moon. Chamulas also believe in individual animal-soul companions that share certain aspects of people's spiritual and physical destinies.

Basic to Chamula cosmology is the belief that they live in the center of the universe (*smišik banamil* or "the navel of the universe"). They believe that their centrality on the square earth-island, combined with their relatively close position to the sun (the highest point in the Chiapas Highlands, Tzontevitz Mountain, 9,500 feet above sea level, lies in Chamula), gives them a special relationship with the sun deity that no other Indian or mestizo community can hope to match. Consequently, they view their home municipio as the only truly safe and virtuous place on the earth. As social distance increases, danger lurks more threateningly. The edges of the earth are populated by demons, strange human beings, and wild animals. From there one can see the terrifying spectacle of the sun and moon deities plunging into and emerging from the seas every day on their respective vertical circuits around the island universe. Not only does the sun deity delimit the spatial limits of the universe, but he also determines the temporal units (days and solar years) by the duration and position of his path. It was the sun who set up order on earth as Chamulas know it. He did this in progressive stages, separately creating the first three worlds and then destroying them, for people behaved improperly. Chamulas say that behavior equivalent to that of the people in the first three creations may still be found at the edges of the universe. It is only the Fourth Creation that has been successful, although

Chamulas still must strive to defend it from bad behavior and evil people. Language, particularly the oral tradition, is a crucial weapon for the defense, continuity, and ritual maintenance of the Chamula universe.

Although the federal government has built over forty primary schools (teaching the first four grades) in Chamula over the past thirty years, hoping thereby to teach Spanish, the community remains linguistically very conservative. Contributing to this conservatism is the fact that only one Ladino (Spanish-speaking) family lives within the municipio boundaries. The 1960 census estimates place the percentage of male bilinguals in Spanish and Tzotzil at 5.52, females at 1.34.[2] Practically speaking, most men know enough Spanish for the basic business of buying and selling and for employment in the Ladino community. However, the growth rate of Chamula (over 4 percent annually) keeps the high percentage of monolingual speakers of Tzotzil remarkably constant in spite of the efforts of the Mexican government.

The Taxonomy of Verbal Behavior

Oral tradition in this conservative community remains vitally and dynamically alive. For the vast majority of Chamulas it is a crucial source of information about the present and the only source of information about the past. Transistor radios are still luxuries possessed by only the wealthy. Even for the few who have radios, the Spanish language (in which all radio programs are broadcast) makes it difficult for them to understand. In short, far from being marginal and moribund, the oral tradition is absolutely critical for maintenance of the social order as Chamulas know it. Consequently, facility in use of ordinary and special forms of language is an ability that nearly all successful political and religious officials and shamans possess.

A bewildering number of processes, abstractions, and things can be glossed as *k'op*, which refers to nearly all forms of verbal behavior, including oral tradition. The term *k'op* can mean the following: word, language, argument, war, subject, topic, problem, dispute, court case, or traditional verbal lore. Chamulas recognize that correct use of language (that is, the Chamula dialect of Tzotzil) distinguishes them not only from nonhumans, but also from their distant ancestors and from other contemporary Indian and Spanish-speaking groups. According to Chamula narrative accounts, no one could speak in the distant past. That was one of the reasons why the sun-creator destroyed the experimental people of the First and Second Creations. The more recent people learned to speak Spanish and then everyone understood one another. Later, the nations and *municipios* were divided because they began quarreling. The sun deity changed languages so that people would learn to live together peacefully in small groups. Chamulas came out well in the long run, for their language was the best of them all (they refer to Tzotzil as *baɗ'i k'op* or "true language"). Language, then, came to be the distin-guishing trait of social groups. It was because of the importance Chamulas attached to correct verbal behavior as a defining trait of their own identity that I considered the range and organization of behavior included in *k'op* to be worthy of detailed attention in my research.

The taxonomy of *k'op,* which follows in Figures 1 and 2, was elicited several separate times from six male informants ranging in age from eighteen to sixty-five over the period of one year. I used both formal question frames and informal discussion to discover these categories. The two methods were complementary, in that formal question frame interviewing (for example, *hay tos*_____?_____ *?oy šaval li Ho?ote,* "How many kinds of_____?_____ would you say there are?") produced a taxonomy and genre labels I could use to identify types of texts after I had recorded or transcribed them (for example, *mi ha?* _____?_____ *lie,* "Is this a _____?_____ ?"). In addition to its utility in providing explicit native genre labels for organizing my collection and being sure of getting comprehensive "coverage," the taxonomy also gave me some needed security and efficiency in helping me develop a specific Tzotzil vocabulary for working with a kind of information my informants took for granted. As important as the taxonomy itself were the clues it suggested for deciding on useful kinds of supporting information I might collect for all texts. Specifically, since time associations of the genres appeared as the principal attribute that distinguished the two supercategories of "pure words" ("recent words" and "ancient words"; see Figures 1 and 2), it occurred to me early in my fieldwork that temporal attributes of the genres might provide a key for understanding the whole of the oral tradition as it related to other aspects of Chamula life and thought. Since I also knew from my interviewing on cosmology that spatial categories originally determined temporal categories (that is, the sun's first vertical trip around the earth set up the categories of day and night, seasons and years) and that time past remained alive at the edges of the universe, I decided I would elicit explicit temporal and spatial data for all texts, in addition to basic informant and contextual data. The relationship of these cosmological variables to oral tradition is discussed in more detail in Figure 3. For the present, a simplified scheme (Fig. 1) and a more detailed taxonomy (Fig. 2) are given.

The two figures should be more or less self-explanatory. The reader will probably note that I have not made an effort to describe the taxonomy as a grid of uniform or symmetrical criteria and distinctive features. Such a scheme would be a distortion of the way in which Chamulas view the taxonomy. For example: time is a relevant criterial attribute for distinguishing level 3 categories of "new words" and "recent words"; for other categories at the same level (3) of the taxonomy, place of performance is a defining feature ("court speech"); for still others at the same level (3), performer of the words is the relevant feature ("children's improvised games"). Therefore, although I use the term "level" in referring to the scheme, I do not attach any uniform "deep structure" information to it. Levels are used only as descriptive conventions. Although I frequently recorded taxa at level 5 in the field, I have not recorded them in this abbreviated version of the classification because responses at this level were far

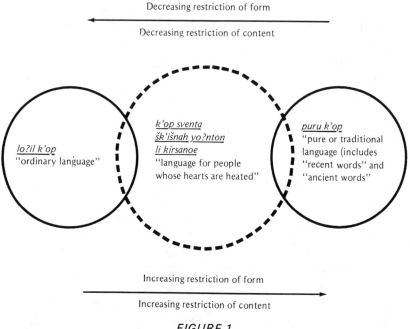

Decreasing restriction of form

Decreasing restriction of content

lo?il k'op
"ordinary language"

k'op sventa
šk'išnah yo?nton
li kirsanoe
"language for people
whose hearts are heated"

puru k'op
"pure or traditional
language (includes
"recent words" and
"ancient words"

Increasing restriction of form

Increasing restriction of content

FIGURE 1
A BRIEF SCHEME OF A FOLK TAXONOMY
OF CHAMULA VERBAL BEHAVIOR

from uniform from informant to informant. I include level 5 items in a few of the brief genre descriptions below, but only when the majority of my informants recognized them. Much more useful than any abstract explanatory grid one might impose on the taxonomy are the Chamula explanations of the supercategories. These are included in Figure 2.

"Ordinary language" (*lo?il k'op*) is restricted in use only by the dictates of the social situation and grammaticality or intelligibility of the utterance. It is believed to be totally idiosyncratic and without noteworthiness in style, form, or content; it is everyday speech. As one moves from left to right in Figures 1 and 2, progressively more constraints of various sorts are apparent in what a person says (content) and how he says it (form). The intermediate category ("language for people whose hearts are heated") contains kinds of verbal behavior that are neither "ordinary language" nor "pure

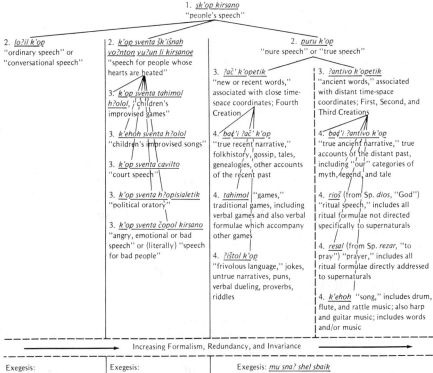

FIGURE 2
A FOLK TAXONOMY OF CHAMULA VERBAL BEHAVIOR

words." They are restricted with regard to form (that is, how people will speak), but they are unpredictable as far as content is concerned. A common Chamula explanation for this kind of emotional speech emphasizes the individual, idiosyncratic qualities of the performance: "It comes from the heart of each person." The term referring to all of these intermediate forms, "language for people whose hearts are heated," implies an elevated, excited, but not necessarily religious attitude on the part of the speaker. This state of excitement produces a style of verbal behavior in the intermediate forms that also occurs in the genres of "true words." Yet, because content in the former depends on the individual whim of the speaker, these forms are not included by Chamulas as a part of "pure words." It is only with the joint presence of prescribed content and prescribed form in genres to which all people ideally have equal access that we reach "pure words" on the right-hand side of the continuum shown in Figures 1 and 2. As Chamulas told me, " 'pure words' do not know how to change." In a sense, then, the heat metaphor, which implies a transition into a more stylized form of speech, continues from the intermediate category into the domain of "pure words," which contains the "genuine" Chamula genres of oral tradition. The implication is an obvious but, I believe, important one: Chamula oral tradition ("pure words") is only a part of a continuum of styles of verbal behavior occurring in other, less standardized contexts. The classes of verbal behavior that are transitional carry vital information for making sense of what is "pure words." Furthermore, Chamula children begin to learn some of the transitional forms (particularly improvised games and songs and emotional speech) long before they begin to experiment with "pure words." It therefore seems crucial to consider the whole of verbal behavior rather than just those genres having constant form and content. This will be discussed in greater detail below.

Within "pure words," the criterion of time association is the most important one in distinguishing the secular forms ("recent words," associated with the present Fourth Creation) from those having greater ritual and etiological significance ("ancient words," associated with the First, Second, and Third Creations). Several apparent discrepancies in the scheme strike the non-Chamula observer. For example, it is highly probable that certain stylistic features of "ancient words" may also be found in verbal aspects of "children's improvised games," which are thought to be idiosyncratic expressions of individual whims in the present. (Repetition of a single pattern of syntax four to six times, with substitution of only one new word for every repetition is a common feature of both "children's improvised games" and "true ancient narrative.") This does not constitute an internal inconsistency in the taxonomy, but rather illustrates a simple notion that is too often ignored: children probably would not be able to recognize, understand, or learn the formal genres of "ancient words" if they did not experiment with the content, styles, rhythms, and syntax in their informal play behavior.

Another example of apparent inconsistency is also instructive. Gossip might seem to the American or European observer to be excluded from anyone's oral tradition, for it cannot become truly "traditional" overnight. Tradition is, however, a relative thing. In Chamula, gossip does belong to "pure speech" most of the time. Gossip, as the Chamulas see it, is not idiosyncratic or original in the way that intermediate types of verbal behavior are. Gossip is part of "true recent narrative" because it is a statement of fact, a segment of information known by several people in a single form, which ideally will be passed on as a whole. All, theoretically, have equal access to it. To illustrate: the gossip among women at a waterhole about the chief magistrate's oration to the Chamulas at a past festival is "true recent narrative," whereas the oration itself is not. The oration ("political oratory") belongs to the transitional category of "speech for people whose hearts are heated" because no one knew what he was going to say, only how he would say it. Another illustration may help to clarify the taxonomic criteria. Emotional speech ("speech for bad people") uses devices of cadence, repetition, syntax, and metaphor that are also found in "pure words." However, it is not considered "pure words" unless a murder or some other noteworthy event follows the quarrel in which the "speech for bad people" was used. In that case the murder, together with the language used, would probably be worthy of retelling as "true recent narrative."

Brief Genre Descriptions and Illustrations

It is now time to offer brief descriptions and illustrations of the genres. After this, I shall discuss them as a unit again, for the whole tells considerably more about Chamula society and thought than any one or even the sum of the parts. The whole behaves as an impressive information system which is logically tied to Chamula cosmology and world view. However, the role of each part should be briefly clarified. Parts A, B, and C below refer to the second-level taxa in Figure 2.

A. *"Ordinary speech"*

This has been discussed above. Here let me repeat simply that this is conventional speech. No one thinks about it as a special form, except to contrast the "correct" Chamula dialect with the "incorrect" neighboring Tzotzil dialects. It has no restrictions as to form and content except that it be intelligible, grammatical, and appropriate.

B. *"Speech for people whose hearts are heated"*

Generally speaking, these intermediate forms of emotional speech contain predictable stylistic devices but do not contain predictable content. They can be said to be idiosyncratic.

1. *"Children's improvised games"*

These games, including verbal and nonverbal components alike, tend usually to be imperfect children's imitations of adult behavior. They are distinct from "games" which belong to "recent words" (below) because the latter have rules which are predictable and obligatory from one performance to the next. "Children's improvised games" do not behave in this way. Typical examples are small boys' imitations of their fathers' ritual behavior and everyday tasks in the corn field. Little girls between two and four also imitate their mothers' weaving and tortilla-making. Parents do not criticize these imperfect imitations, but neither do they recognize them as standard "games." Parents frequently say, regarding these forms of play, that "they come from the heart of each one." The most typical verbal component of these games is also related to language learning. It is verbatim repetition of phrases, often three or four times. For example, as a child pretends to herd imaginary sheep he may yell:

lok' an!   *lok' an!*   *lok' an!*
Get out!   Get out!   Get out!

This form of repetition is related not only to the other forms of "speech for people whose hearts are heated," but also the genres of "pure words," as we shall see below.

2. *"Children's improvised songs"*

These songs, like the games above, are imperfect children's imitations of "song," a genre that occurs in "pure words." The most typical content of these songs is a child's narration of what he is doing as he is playing or working. One reason adults exclude these songs from the "proper" class of "song" is that "song" is ideally used only for ritual contexts. This ideal is constantly abused by adults themselves, who use the religious music in numerous secular contexts. However, the crucial difference appears to be that adults know the right tunes to go with the right words; children do not. Furthermore, most children cannot play the instruments (harp and guitar) that should accompany "song." Therefore, even though children use the "right" melody (form) with improvised words (content), adults do not accept it as legitimate "song."

An important linguistic component of "children's improvised song" is experimentation with metaphoric couplets, which are the most important stylistic building blocks of the formal genres of "ancient words." For example, the following song line came from a child's song of speculation about what animal soul he had. The small boy (four years old) sang it as he struck a cat with a stick:

> *pinto čon un bi.*
> spotted animal (you are)
>
> *pinto bolom un bi.*
> spotted jaguar (you are)

The melody was "correct" and even the words could conceivably occur in a true "song," called *Bolom Čon* ("Jaguar

Animal"), but the child's attitude was incorrect. He was idly looking at a domestic cat and was presumptuously speculating that he, as a mere child, might have an animal soul companion as powerful as the jaguar, who, everyone knows, is the animal soul companion only of rich and powerful adults. Furthermore, it was not sung in any semblance of a ritual context. The performance was therefore imperfect on several counts. However, the couplet which is cited above has a structure like hundreds which exist in more formal genres: same syntax in two lines, with a one-word synonym substitution in the second line.

3. "Court speech"

"Court speech" refers to the language used by political officials, defendants, plaintiffs, and witnesses at court hearings that occur every day of the year except fiesta days. Verbal competence is absolutely crucial to anyone's success in court. Emotions, of course, play a vital part in all court happenings. The stylistic canons for "heated hearts" are nearly always apparent in "court speech." However, because each case is theoretically unique, one does not know what people will say, only how they will say it. The outstanding stylistic traits of "court speech" are metaphoric couplets (discussed above) and parallel syntax. The following example of parallel syntax is taken from the chief magistrate's condemnation of a woman who had been caught red-handed with stolen sheep. Note that the repeated syntax, with one word substitutions, is related to the metaphoric couplet and serves as an intensifier of the message. The magistrate's heart is very much heated.

?oy ša shayibuk velta šavelk' anik
Many times already you have stolen!

šavelk'an li čihe;	šavelk'an ti ?alak'e
You steal sheep;	you steal chickens!
šavelk'an ti ?isak'e;	šavelk'an ti ma?ile
You steal potatoes;	you steal squash!

šavelk'an ti k'u ?ile;	*šavelk'an ti ?itahe*
You steal clothing;	you steal cabbage!
šavelk'an ti tuluk'e;	*skotol k'usi šavelk'an*
You steal turkeys;	you steal anything!

?a ? ša no ?oš muyuk bu šavelk'anbe sbek'yat li kirsanoetik
The only thing you don't steal from people are their testicles;

?a? no?oš čalo?
And those you only eat!

The redundant style helps to make the last line more embarrassing for the defendant, for it accuses her of oral-genital contact, which is disapproved of as animal-like; it is a metaphoric restatement of the animal-like qualities of her habitual thievery which have just been stated in parallel structures nine times. We will see below that, although this speech is idiosyncratic in content, the form of redundancy and parallelism is repeated throughout the oral tradition.

4. *"Political oratory"*

"Political oratory" includes all public announcements made by religious and political officials outside ritual settings. Like "court speech," "political oratory" has highly predictable stylistic components; yet each performance is theoretically different, which is why it does not qualify as "pure speech." Since the stylistic devices that characterize it have already been discussed above—parallel syntax, metaphoric couplets, redundancy of message, verbatim repetition—no example will be given.

5. *"Speech for bad people"*

The Chamula term for this genre is somewhat misleading, for this category of speech really refers to any heated, emotional, drunken, or angry discussion. Heat is ideally desirable, for it is an aspect of sacred symbols, including the sun-creator himself. It is when heat gets out of control that Chamulas condemn it. This dual aspect of the heat metaphor is implied by the diversity of attitudes included in the class of "speech for people whose hearts are heated." "Court speech" can be desirable in that it defends the community's well-being. However, "speech for bad people" can very easily lead to machete fights and killings. Therefore, emotional and excited speech can be desirable if controlled and used in defense of the norm; it is undesirable if uncontrolled and used offensively against the norm. "Speech for bad people" thus refers to the language of those whose hearts heat up to the point of no control.

The characteristic linguistic forms of this uncontrolled, emotional speech are as follows: multiple metaphoric restatements that may be in couplet form but also in the form of longer restatements of sentence length, parallel syntax with one- and two-word substitutions, and simple verbatim repetition. Like other forms of the intermediate class, individual performances are unique and theoretically cannot be repeated.

C. "Pure words"

"Pure words" includes those genres having constraints of three types: form, content, and social setting. "Pure words" includes the stable genres of Chamula oral tradition. As a unit, "pure words" carries a veritable arsenal of defense for the Chamula way of life. Part of the strength of these genres seems to relate to the fact that the cyclical view of time, the very underpinning of the Chamula view of cosmic order, serves as an attribute that both unifies "pure words" and subdivides it into two major classes, "recent words" and "ancient words." "Recent words" were learned or acquired in the present, Fourth Creation; "ancient words" were learned in, or acquired in, or refer to the First, Second, and Third Creations. Generally speaking, "recent words" assume the present social order in Chamula and they are preserved and taught by informal means. "Ancient words" relate to the coming and formal maintenance of the Chamula social order. As such, "ancient words" provide the formulas and mythical precedents for ritual action. In order to appreciate the meaning of the temporal dimensions of this part of the taxonomy, it should be remembered that Chamulas do not subscribe to a "Golden Age" view of the past.

The First, Second, and Third Creations were chaotic and difficult times for the inhabitants of the earth. Being imperfect, they were destroyed by the sun-creator. It is only with the present Fourth Creation that the sun-creator (Christ) is pleased. And even in this Creation it is only the Chamulas who know correct behavior according to the sun's will. Other people on earth still practice some of the barbarities of the first three creations. Chamulas think that the three destructions were incomplete at the edges of the earth and that people there preserve various kinds of asocial behavior long ago surpassed by the Chamulas. It is not unlike the European view of human social evolution in the late nineteenth century: those most unlike Europe and living far away were savages; those intermediate in customs and social distance were barbarians; those most like Europeans, living at the center of the universe, enjoyed true civilization. The others might catch up someday. This is precisely the way Chamulas view their universe, but they are not so arrogant as the Europeans were. They believe that the human condition, particularly in Chamula, is very desirable but also very fragile. Every technique must be used to preserve its integrity. "Pure words" help enormously in this endeavor.

1. "Recent words: true recent narrative"

"True recent narrative" includes "true" narrative accounts of Fourth Creation events that are worth repeating as a unit and to which all ideally have equal access. The historical depth of the Fourth Creation is not standard. For some it goes back only to the time of their grandfathers. For others it goes back to a nebulous time, long ago, when there were already good (that is, Chamula) people on earth. Generally speaking, the period refers to a time not radically unlike the present in terms of distribution of people, customs, and languages. In nearly all cases, "true recent narrative" tells of threats to the social order; famines, epidemics, natural disasters, depletion of natural resources; wars, political disputes, foreign intrusions into Chamula territory; immoral Chamulas, evil Ladinos; pranks and punishments attributed to supernaturals; gossip about corrupt officials, murders, theft, moral decay; changing lineage alliances. Nearly all carry a moral: look what happened when people behaved improperly. Only rarely is a genuinely positive event preserved as "true recent narrative." An example is genealogical history (seldom deeper than four generations), in which some ancestor is praised for living uprightly and leaving the present generation a lot of land. No one owns the narratives, nor is there any restriction as to where and when they may be told or who may be present. Narratives are presented as evidence and are told only as appropriate circumstances dictate or as answers to questions and inquiries. For example, accounts of misfortunes associated with droughts would be told if a drought threatened. Chamulas do not have tale-telling sessions as such. Even gossip, which includes many "true recent narratives," is told ostensibly to inform others of recent threats to and changes in the established order. Few tell of personal good fortune, for that would invite accusations of witchcraft. In sum, "true recent narrative" is a kind of catalogue of the human dilemma.

Stylistic traits of "true recent narrative" are familiar continuities from "speech for people whose hearts are heated." However, the joint presence of these traits with fixed content that is supposedly true qualifies these narratives as a genre of "pure words." Individuals may add emphasis in the telling of the event, but they should stick to the facts. There is a device, the greater or lesser density of "stacking" of metaphoric couplets, which serves speakers and listeners as a measure of what in the narrative is judged to be important and what is trivial. Greater redundancy of an idea, in the form of metaphoric couplets, parallel syntax or longer semantic restatement, underlines the importance of the idea. The example which follows illustrates typical composition and a point of emphasis in a single couplet based on parallel syntax.

The following fragment, from a text entitled "The Time of the Fever," tells of the influenza epidemic of 1918, which followed the Mexican Revolution.

veno
Well, then,

k'alal ?ital ti k' ak'al čamel ti vonee
When the fever came long ago

pero veno ha? la smul ti hkaransa
It was because of the crimes of the *carrancistas.*

?iliktal tahmek ta ?olon ?osil
It came from the Hot Country.

la la ščik'ik tal ti htotike
Our Father, the Sun, brought it upon them

la la ščik'ik tal ti santoetike
The saints called it down upon them.

pere ?ora tana ?un
But then something else happened.

2. *"Recent words: frivolous language"*

What "true recent narrative" accomplishes with prose accounts of true breaches of the social order, "frivolous language" accomplishes with laughter. The genre actually consists of five subgenres (which might be called fifth-level taxa in the context of Figure 2). All of these express or refer to ambiguous or deviant behavior, and all elicit laughter from participants and onlookers. Laughter appears to underline the norm by placing the deviant or ambiguous item of behavior in sharp relief against the norm. Using this technique, they effect social control in informal settings and also in formal settings, when other means are not applicable. In all of the subgenres of "frivolous language" stylistic constraints are rigid and great emphasis is given to multiple meanings. Form, content, social setting, and range of alternative meanings are more or less

constant, thus qualifying them for inclusion in "pure words."
Very brief descriptions of the genres are given below.

a) *"Lies" (hut k'op)*. "Lies are prose jokes which tell
of admittedly untrue events. The subgenre might be glossed as
a "tall tale." Nearly always there is a superficial theme which
makes the "lie" sound like "true recent narrative," but there is
always a second, usually sexual, theme which lies beneath the
apparent surface theme. This form is popular boys' joking
behavior and requires considerable linguistic competence for
telling and appreciation. The second meaning usually involves
some item of deviant behavior such as copulation with
animals, adultery, or premarital promiscuity. The laughter
which "lies" elicit emphasizes by contrast what the norm is
and should be. "Lies" share almost all stylistic traits with
"true recent narrative." The difference lies in the verity of the
events reported and in the semantic dimension.

b) *"Genuine frivolous talk" (baƚ'i ʔištol loʔil)*. This
most widely used subgenre of "frivolous language" consists of
hundreds of fixed sets of suggestive words and phrases that
have minimal sound shifts from one to the next. Words or
phrases are spoken alternately by two players as a form of
verbal dueling. The player who cannot respond to a challenge
loses. As in "lies" there is a surface meaning and a second or
more meanings. It is a characteristic form of boys' and men's
joking behavior and frequently accompanies bantering about
sexuality and sexual fantasies in this rather straight-laced
society. It also accompanies some overt homosexual behavior
permitted of adolescents and young men. "Genuine frivolous
talk" requires a great deal of finesse with the language, both
for performance and appreciation. As such, it serves as a
training ground for aspiring politicians and religious officials.
It is a form in which young boys strive to achieve excellence,
for skill with language is highly prized and respected. It
behaves in a way not unlike "signifying" and "ranking" in
black communities in the United States.

An example follows. Note that only one phoneme shift
occurs, but that the shift carries with it a powerful pun. This

fragment is a part of a fixed series that can run to as many as forty exchanges.

> Player I: *?ak'bun ?aviš*
> Give me your older sister.
>
> Player II: *?ak'bo ?aviš*
> Give it to your sister.

The first line implies a request for Player II's older sister's sexual services. The complex meaning relates to the fragility of the brother-in-law relationship in Chamula. In the first place, the players are potential brothers-in-law. In the second place, the relationship is a difficult one, for although a bride-price is always given to the bride's family by the groom's family, she moves to her husband's hamlet to live. This causes bad feelings between the families. Therefore, the request for his sister's free premarital sexual services is preposterous and potentially dangerous and, hence, funny. However, Player II "one-ups" Player I by suggesting that he have sexual relations with his own older sister instead of with Player II's older sister. Incest, of course, is a greater offense than premarital promiscuity. Much that is proscribed in Chamula society is thus underlined and reinforced by the laughter generated by verbal dueling.

c) "Obscure words" (k'ehel k'op). Although glossed as "proverb," this subgenre of "frivolous language" has a different nature and apparently more complex role than proverbs have in Western societies. Ultimately, Chamula "obscure words" make normative statements, but they do this by suggestion, never by actual explicit statement. In fact, they will often state the opposite of the norm. The reason for this is that their social setting demands circumlocution. There are many barriers (such as sex, affinal relationship, age, rank) which make it difficult or impossible for people to address one another freely in many social settings, public and private. Yet when some form of deviant behavior takes place, even in a public setting, the most inferior child may call down an offending elder by using "obscure words." Because they imply normative deviation by metaphor and try indirectly to correct it, and because the referent situation is usually obvious to offender, speaker, and others, they are remarkably funny. Both linguistic form and range of possible referent situations are more or less constant. An example follows:

ta štal li Ho?e	*pere la štakih ta ?ora.*
It is going to rain,	but it will soon dry up.

The deviant addressed was (in the specific performance I witnessed) an old woman who, by pretending to squat innocently under the cover of her long skirt, was actually fouling sacred space in the Ceremonial Center by urinating there surreptitiously. A young man called her down by using this "obscure word." The rain referred to her improper voiding in a public place; the drying up was a suggestion that she go elsewhere. If stated directly, the criticism could have earned him a court case, fine, and jail sentence. As it was, the old woman suffered considerable embarrassment, the crowd got a laugh, and the moral order was upheld.

d) "Riddles" (hak'om k'op). Chamula riddles behave as jokes and nearly always involve double meanings, usually emphasizing sexual or ambivalent topics which are points of stress in Chamula society. They are generally of two types, classified by linguistic form: fixed formulas and prose. In both cases, the form and content are more or less fixed, although the ambiguous referents (that is "possible answers") may fluctuate within a given range of alternatives. An example of the formulaic form follows:

Question: *hme? kumagre haval*
My comadre is face-up,

kumpagre nuhul
My compadre is face-down.

k'usi ?un
What is it?

Answer: *teša*
A roof tile.

Ceramic roof tiles are arranged on alternate rafters in curved-side-up, curved-side-down interlocking sequence; hence the sexual pun. The reference to the sex life of one's ritual kin (from Spanish *compadres*, "coparents") is ordinarily improper, for one should have a strict respect relationship with them. The "riddle" actually emphasizes the importance of this respectful ritual relationship, which is a potential source of loans, labor, and general support. This fact is possibly expressed metaphorically in the image of the tile, a roof material that is expensive and better than thatching, for it affords better rain protection and lasts longer. The tile is thus analogous to the *compadrazgo* relationship, which costs something to establish but gives security in return. It should therefore be treated with respect. The humor generated by the "riddle" emphasizes this. The prose form of "riddles" deals with similar topics, but the question asked is stated in a longer and more involved way.

e) "Buried words (mukul k'op).   This subgenre behaves as a prose riddle but is usually used to refer to specific situations, to describe and control specific cases of normative deviation. It uses the familiar parallel structures, discussed above, but the key words are nearly always sexual or scatological puns. Like "obscure words," "buried words" frequently call attention to some error in personal appearance or behavior. In a sense they tell an offender what is "wrong" by involving him in a suggestive guessing game. The humor underlines the norm but also mitigates potential hard feelings and quarrels.

3. "Recent words: games"

This genre includes verbal and nonverbal aspects of those games having definite rules and names. It is sometimes divided further into children's games, which are combined verbal and nonverbal performances, and adults' games, which are mostly verbal. The latter overlap with the subgenre of "frivolous language." Space does not permit full discussion of these games, but in reference to children's games, it is important to note that they include rule-governed action of both a verbal and nonverbal nature. This implies that the verbal/nonverbal distinction is not particularly significant to Chamulas. It is rather the rule-governed aspect, the moral dimension, the predictability, which matter as criteria for inclusion of the genre in "pure words." Most Chamula children's games assign roles to players according to relative age. The older children have more authority and more "human" roles; the younger children have roles more appropriate to their lesser experience in the rule-governed universe. The themes of the games usually concern important social category distinctions, such as people and demons, people and animals, good people and bad people. The themes attempt to duplicate category relationships in Chamula society. Thus, rank coexists with equality and very seldom are there "winners" in any sort of free competition.

The verbal component is usually a combination of fixed lines of emotional speech and set formulas. The emotion lines accompanying the action are verbatim repetitions (usually in twos and threes) of key words and phrases. Frequently there are also set phrases, which must be said to make the game "correct." One such line comes from a kind of hide-and-go-seek game called Peter Lizard (*petul ?okoȼ'*) in which the child playing Peter Lizard hides, while the other children try to find him, shouting:

> *buyot*   *buyot*
> Where are you?   Where are you?
>
> *buyot, petul ?okoȼ'*
> Where are you, Peter Lizard?

When they find him (he helps by giving whistle signals), they pursue him and eventually trap him by piling on top of him. Thus, both actions and speech have constraints of form and content in true Chamula "games."

4. *"Ancient words: true ancient narrative"*

This narrative genre shares many stylistic traits and performance aspects with "true recent narrative" (see above). The important difference between the two is content, this being related to the temporal dimension. Like all genres of "ancient words," "true ancient narrative" reports or refers to events of the first three creations. As such, most of the narrations are etiological and explanatory. They tell of the origin of the earth, people, animals, customs. They include numerous anecdotes about the way life was in the first three creations; how animals, people, and inanimate objects could talk; how animals tricked one another; how all of these interacted with supernaturals. Chamulas often divide this genre into three subgenres: accounts of the First, Second, and Third Creations. Events, of course, become progressively more like modern Chamula life as one progresses from the First to the Third Creation. There are no prescribed settings for telling these tales.

Related to the role of "true ancient narrative" in stating the coming of the present order is a greater message redundancy than one finds in "true recent narrative." This greater density of metaphoric couplets and parallel structures, which I call "metaphoric stacking," appears to be related to a tendency for narrators to use greater redundancy for emphasis. Items of assumed knowledge about the nature of order appear to require more of this emphasis than the threats to order which are reported in "true recent narrative." An example of this pattern follows. It is a fragment from a narrative about the Second Creation relating the origin of Ladinos from the offspring of a Second Creation Ladino woman and her dog. Note the symmetry of this fragment, built of couplets.

	šinulan ?anƭ
parallel	The Ladino woman,
couplet	
	ˇsinulan ƭeb
	The Ladino girl;

	k'uyepal ?oy
interrogative couplet	How many were there?
	čib sbi
	Two of them.

	ḓ'akal ta šanav
parallel couplet	Behind her it walked,
	ḓ'akal ta sbe?in
	Behind her it travelled;

	šč?uk sḓ'i?
semantic couplet	She and the dog,
	muyuk bu ta šanav stuk
	She did not walk alone.

Not all texts are as symmetrical and redundant as this one, nor is symmetry necessarily present throughout a text. The fragment, however, illustrates a general tendency for all genres of "ancient words" to utilize greater stylistic redundancy than "recent words." This relates to the kind of information carried; it is crucial, basic knowledge that must be understood by all and formally maintained.

5. "Ancient words: prayer"

"Prayer" is ritual language addressed to supernaturals. It consists wholly of formal, bound couplets. I have never heard a "prayer" composed of smaller elements. Its use implies a ritual setting. All adult Chamulas know some "prayers"; religious specialists know hundreds. In all cases the components remain the same: highly redundant, metaphoric couplets with prescribed content and a more or less fixed order, the content and order of the couplets being determined by the specific ritual setting.

An example follows. It is a fragment from a layman's "prayer" of salutation to the image of San Juan (Chamula's patron saint) in the Chamula church.

muk'ta san huan

parallel
couplet

Great San Juan,

muk'ta patron
Great patron,

lital ta yolon ?avok

parallel
couplet

I have come before your feet;

lital ta yolon ?ak'ob
I have come before your hands;

šči?uk hnup

parallel
couplet

With my wife,

šči?uk hči ?il
With my companion,

šči?uk kol

parallel
couplet

With my children,

šči?uk hnič'on
With my offspring.

This text illustrates a pattern of "ancient words": that the greater the symbolic significance of a transaction, the more condensed and redundant will be the language used to conduct it.

6. "Ancient words: ritual speech"

"Ritual speech" includes all ritual language not directed to supernaturals. Like "prayer," all adult Chamulas must know some kinds of "ritual speech"; religious and political specialists know the dozens of kinds required for their respective tasks. "Ritual speech" is used by ritual officials and laymen to talk among themselves on the elevated plane of the ritual setting. It is constantly present in Chamula life, from drinking ceremonies to installation of new ritual officials to bride-petitioning rites. Since it always accompanies ritual transactions, its content is as varied as these settings. The style (with some exceptions, such as drinking toasts) is very much like that of "prayer," and it is remarkably constant from one setting to the next. Like "prayer," it is built almost entirely of bound formal couplets, which are theoretically irreducible components for the composition of "ritual speech." The relationship of redundancy of style and content to the high symbolic significance of the transaction applies to "ritual speech" as it does to "prayer."

7. "Ancient words: song"

"Song" may be seen as the opposite end of a continuum of formalism and redundancy beginning with "ordinary language" (lo?il k'op). "Song" has all of the formal stylistic attributes of "prayer" and "ritual speech," plus musical form and instrumental accompaniment. "Song" is present at nearly all Chamula public rituals and at most private ones. No major Chamula ritual performance takes place without musicians. (Holy Week festivities are a near exception to this rule.) "Song" is a form of language addressed to supernaturals or giving them information about the progress of a ritual. As such, "song" should not ideally be secular. But in practice it is widely used in secular settings. The ritual content in the lyrics, however, is not changed in secular settings in which I have seen and heard "song" performed. Pieces with words (which musicians and ritual officials sing to the accompaniment of harp, guitar, and rattle) and without words (played on drum and flute and, occasionally, on horn, accordion, and ocarina by specialists for certain major fiestas) are classed as "song" (k'ehoh). The instruments are said to sing just as people do. "Song" is an extreme statement of redundancy, for the musical form and couplet structure make it possible to repeat them *ad infinitum* until the ritual events they accompany have concluded. An example follows. It is a fragment from a "song" for one of the ritual officials in charge of San Juan's cult.

parallel couplet	*sk'ak'alil ?ak'inale* It is the day of your fiesta!
	sk'ak'alil ?apaškue It is the day of your celebration!
parallel couplet	*muk'ulil san huane* Great San Juan,
	muk'ulil patrone Great Patron.
parallel couplet	*k'uyepal čihšanavotik ?o ta hlikel bi* How soon we are to begin walking!
	k'uyepal čihsanavotik ?o ta htabel bi How soon we will be taking you in procession!
parallel couplet	*sk'ak'alil ?aničim ba* It is the day of your flowery countenance,
	sk'ak'alil ?aničim sat It is the day of your flowery face.
nonsense syllables as parallel structures	*la la li la lai la ?o* *la la li la lai la ?a* *la la li la lai la ?a* *la la li la lai la ?o*

Genres and Cosmos

The time has come to try to pull some of the pieces back together. It has been my argument throughout that there is more that holds Chamula oral tradition together, as a reservoir of knowledge, than separates it into diverse genres. It makes more sense together, for that is the way it is learned, used, and even changed.

In this section, I should like to argue that a metalanguage of time and space binds together the normative, the credible, and the desirable in oral tradition as the same categories of time and space hold the moral universe together (as discussed above). That this might be the case should come as no surprise, for language is viewed by Chamulas as a distinctively human trait, which occurs in its perfect form in the Chamula dialect of Tzotzil (*baq'i k'op,* the "true language"). It should rather come as a surprise if the organization of linguistic information about the universe did not show a significant relationship to the structure of the universe itself. The taxonomy (Fig. 2) suggests that time is indeed a relevant variable to consider, for "pure words" are themselves divided into "ancient words" and "recent words," according to their associations in the First through Fourth Creations. Even "ordinary speech" and "speech for people whose hearts are heated" have a neutral temporal dimension in that they are ephemeral phenomena of the Fourth Creation; they do not have predictable form and content.

What do the present and the past mean in terms of space? Chamulas constantly insisted that behavior that had been surpassed by Chamulas after the First, Second, and Third Creations still survived at the edges of their spatial universe. This suggested that time and space were aspects of the same cosmological reality, just as they were in the beginning when the sun-creator initiated the First Creation and all later temporal categories with his first spatial orbit around the universe. It therefore seemed reasonable to suppose that the order-giving and order-maintaining information in the oral tradition might demonstrate the same time-space unity. To examine this further, I compared the temporal and spatial variables of 184 texts of "true recent narrative" and "true ancient narrative." On a simple graph I plotted values of the time each narrative had taken place with the most distant place-name mentioned in the same text. These specific temporal and spatial data as well as genre label were elicited for each text (discussed above). The time axis began with the present and went progressively back to the First Creation. The space axis began with Chamula and had categories of space increasingly unlike Chamula and socially distant (Gossen 1970:365). Results indicated that Chamula beliefs about the universe were clearly replicated in both the taxonomy and the content of their narratives. Events that took place in the Fourth Creation and belonged to "true recent narrative"; events that took place in progressively more distant spatial categories of the universe also took place, progressively, in the Third, Second, and First Creations. Extrapolated from the narrative genres to all genres, this suggests that analogous values of time and space work together as dimensions of logic, credibility, and function in Chamula oral tradition. I also suggest that these same dimensions may regulate change in and accretions to the oral tradition.

A summary of the covariation I suggest appears in Figure 3. The center of the octagonal diagram represents Chamula. It is to be read either outward from or inward toward the center. In any one of the eight sections, at any point between the center and outer line of the diagram, a line can be traced around the other sections at points equidistant from the center. The line so described will show points of association of the eight dimensions with one another. The diagram attempts to show aspects of cosmology and world view that appear to be intimately and systematically related to Chamula genres of verbal behavior. The outermost segment of the diagram suggests aspects of "antistructure" (to borrow from Victor Turner) which may be used against the moral order by the antisocial forces of the universe.

Summary and Conclusions

Chamula oral tradition is not only associated with norms but also actively involved in teaching, reinterpreting, and maintaining them. "Recent words" and "speech for people whose hearts are heated" teach and enforce by relatively informal means in the present the moral order that "ancient words" maintain by ritual means and formal explanations

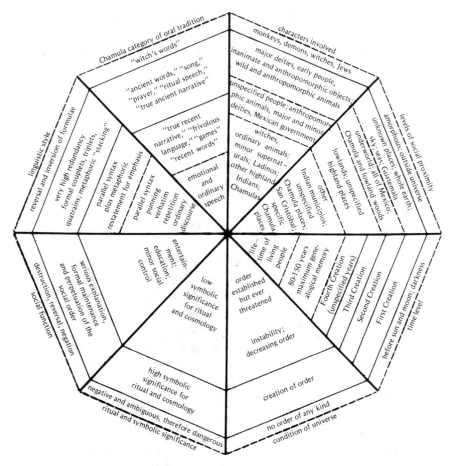

FIGURE 3
A MODEL OF SOME ASPECTS OF CHAMULA ORAL TRADITION
AND COSMOLOGY

reaching back in time. It should not be surprising that fundamental social categories like time and space bear a relationship to the content, categories, function, and style of traditional verbal behavior. Language is, after all, a social fact *par excellence*. Oral tradition in Chamula is a crucial aspect of language. Taken separately, Chamula genres are but fragments of the totality of specialized verbal competence successful adults must master. The whole carries more information than the sum of the parts. In a nut shell, then, this paper makes a case for looking at the whole in addition to the parts. Some implications follow:

First, if our consideration of Chamula oral tradition were restricted to what we call myth, folktales, legend, folk music, or pun, we could hope for no more than a distorted view of the collective representations of the community. These Western genres are not significant, as such, in Chamula. Furthermore, even if they were significant to Chamulas, these few "standard genres" would account for no more than a fraction of the vast amount of information contained in the many classes of Chamula verbal behavior. For example, to attempt to understand Chamula religion and cosmology using "true ancient narrative" alone would present distortions similar to those that might come from discussing a kinship system without discussing the terms below "ego" or the terms for affines. In kinship studies, anthropologists make every effort to emphasize the culture-specific meaning of kin terms within a whole system. Why not do the same for verbal behavior? This perspective might introduce some much-needed caution into the cross-cultural "comparative method" as it is frequently found in folklore studies.

Second, my Chamula data show that no genre of "pure words" has any special logical primacy over any other genre for purposes of analysis. There is as much information about cosmology and social categories in a recent item of gossip in "true recent narrative" as there is in an item of "ritual speech." The form is simply different. This calls into question the inordinate amount of attention anthropologists have consistently given to myth and ritual. The "minor" genres, if noted, might supply the same information—perhaps in less cryptic form than the formal genres. They might even provide objective tests for such useful intuitive notions as "nature" and "culture." This would allow us to interpret myth as another code for information that is given explicitly elsewhere in the oral tradition. Such an intracultural comparison of genres offers exciting prospects when combined with such methods as structural analysis.

Third, a holistic approach to Chamula oral tradition permits a useful perspective for observing how children acquire adult verbal competence. The Chamula data indicate that children learn their oral tradition as a stylistic and generic continuum. "Prayer," for example, is a sophisticated form that is learned as a separate form relatively late in childhood and presupposes certain religious information and ability to use parallel syntax style and redundancy. Children learn these things much earlier in their linguistic play with "games" and "frivolous talk." To ignore the whole would be to ignore a very significant dimension of Chamula communication: oral tradition behaves as a system of interpenetrating styles and information.

Finally, a holistic approach helps to emphasize that patterns of ideal behavior are found throughout the cultural fabric, from court procedure to play, from games to ritual, from joking to prayer. A study of these structural patterns offers a comprehensive view of the meaning of esthetic forms, possibly providing an illustration of the old-fashioned idea that esthetics are ethics.

NOTES

1. The research reported in this paper was carried out in Chamula, State of Chiapas, Mexico, between January, 1968, and January, 1969, and also in the summer of 1965, as a part of the Harvard Chiapas Project, a continuing field research center under the direction of Professor Evon Z. Vogt of Harvard University. Intellectual and practical support from him and other participants in the project throughout my research is greatefully acknowledged. In particular, I wish to thank Victoria R. Bricker and Robert Laughlin for their many helpful suggestions while I was in the field. I also thank Professor Munro Edmonson for introducing me to some of the patterns of Quiché Maya oral composition. My fieldwork was supported financially by a National Institute of Mental Health predoctoral fellowship. This version of the paper was first presented at the American Folklore Society Meetings in Los Angeles in 1970. I also wish to thank Roger Abrahams, Richard Bauman, Alan Dundes, Barbara Kirshenblatt-Gimblett, Joel Sherzer, and Brian Stross for their helpful comments. James J. Fox, M. Kirk Endicott and

Michelle Rosaldo also made helpful comments and criticisms of earlier versions of this paper. Summarized here is some of the material from my dissertation in anthropology, "Time and Space in Chamula Oral Tradition" (Gossen 1970).

2. Secretaría de Industria y Comercio, *VIII Censo general de población, 1960, 8 de junio. Estado de Chiapas* (Mexico, D.F., 1963).

REFERENCES CITED

Gossen, Gary H.
    1970   Time and Space in Chamula Oral Tradition. Ph.D. dissertation, Harvard University.
Lévi-Strauss, Claude
    1963   The Structural Study of Myth. *In* Structural Anthropology. New York: Basic Books.

9

THE TRAINING OF THE MAN OF WORDS IN TALKING SWEET[1]

Roger D. Abrahams

As in other parts of Afro-America, on St. Vincent there is a good deal of talk about talk. This reflects a belief that life is to be judged in terms of performances and that talking of any sort is regarded as a performance phenomenon. One is constantly being judged by the way in which he talks or acts, judgment being based upon a sense of agreement between the enactment of a social role and the expectations arising from the social situation.

There are two basic categories of behavior, the *rude* and the *behaved*; the one involves *playing the fool* or *talking nonsense,* the other *talking sensible.* A wide variety of acts and events are categorized and judged in terms of this basic dichotomy. Rudeness is not judged as categorically bad behavior; there are certain ceremonial occasions (like Carnival and wakes) when it is regarded as appropriate and is encouraged. In everyday behavior, however, rudeness and nonsense are responded to as inappropriate, although expected

This essay is reprinted by permission from *Language in Society 1,* 1972, pp. 15-29.

nonetheless, especially of young men. Since [good] *behavior* is often equated with *talking sweet* (speaking close to Standard English) and rudeness with *talking broad,* there is a linguistic dimension to this evaluative procedure. Furthermore, *talking sweet* has come to be identified not so much with the Euro-American world as with peasant household values. In contrast, *talking bad* is identified with male life away from home. The two varieties are recognized as distinct, then, as part of the native cognizance of the social dichotomy between female and male, the household and the crossroads worlds (Abrahams 1970a). This correlates with Peter Wilson's description of the distinction between male canons of *reputation* and the female code of *respectability* (Wilson 1969).

This identification of language variety with a social dichotomy does not mean that women always speak sweetly nor that men always talk bad. These varieties are associated with the value systems of the two groups and do come into conflict occasionally. But most important for our purposes, the *sweet* varieties are associated with ceremonies that celebrate household values, while *talking broad* is stylized for licentious performances.

As part of the training in household values, then, one of the responsibilities of the head of the household is to assure that each of its younger members develops some competence in *talking sweet.* But this cannot always be done by a household member. More characteristically, just as there used to be elegant letter-writers to whom one could go for such a service, especially during courtship, there are those who are renowned in the community for their speechmaking abilities who will give lessons to children sent to them.

There are different kinds of speechmaking occasions involving different degrees of difficulty in the attainment of the speechmaking skills. Naturally, the more elaborate the skill the young person will have to exhibit, the greater the chance that he or she will be sent to one of these men of words. There are essentially two types of speechmaking occasions in which talking sweet will be called for: the home ceremonies like marriage fetes, thanksgiving, baptisms, and send-offs, in which everyone is expected to make a speech or sing a song; and the festival ceremony, like Christmas or Carnival masquerading, the school *concert* or *tea meeting,* in which the more highly trained young people are given a chance to demonstrate their abilities. Of course, these latter occasions call for a speechmaking apprenticeship considerably more involved than the former; and it is for these occasions that the man of words is called on to teach.

Paralleling these two levels of speechmaking difficulty, one may distinguish between two kinds of ceremony in the British West Indies, those which are connected with rites of passage and those which arise during calendrical rites. The former are strongly associated with the maintenance of the family and household system, while the latter gravitate in the opposite direction, toward the acting out of licentious and antisocial feelings. Significantly, the rites of passage are carried on in the house and yard, while the licentious ceremonies are restricted to the country roads, the crossroads areas, and on the big days, the city streets.

It is in the household ceremonies like wedding feasts and send-offs that the smaller speechmaking occurs in which nearly everyone in the group is expected to demonstrate their abilities. The calendrical festivals, on the other hand, are commonly events in which only the most proficient performers hold forth, but even here the performances gravitate away from speaking events toward action-oriented ones like dancing, stilt-walking, acrobatics, mock wars, and various performances which will bring the focus of the audience on the brilliant costuming.

But there are intermediate types of activities, calendrical events which are either carried on in yards along the road, or in buildings other than the home. These events, more public than the licentious festivals but more restricted than the festival, are those in which the great oratorical eloquence traditions arise. Included here is the Christmas serenading common throughout this culture area, in which songs alternate with praise orations given by the man of words included in the performing group especially for that purpose. Here too are the acting groups, the Carnival play *mas'* (masquerade) troupes or the Christmas mumming groups who play scenes from Shakespeare or *Pilgrim's Progress* or the St. George and the Turk play. And here also are the *tea meeting* orators, the fledgling men of words who come together to test out their eloquent skills in competition with each other and with the rudeness and nonsense of the audience (Abrahams 1970b).

The distinction between the two types of ceremony is paralleled by differences in the language variety commonly employed and the value systems symbolized by the variety employed. The household ceremony utilizes eloquence traditions which equate oratorical and elaborate speechmaking abilities with the continuing order and respectability of the household. The speeches engendered by these occasions overtly discuss the necessity of family order, responsibility and continuity. The language variety thereby comes to be identified with the canons of respect and family maintenance. Therefore, when everyone is expected to make their oral contribution to the eloquent proceedings, they are each being asked to make a declaration in favor of the family values appropriate to the household setting and the occasion.

By contrast, the licentious performances employ an emphatically creole, broken manner of expression, *talking broad* presented dramatically. This, when coupled with the stylized and permitted rudeness of such performances (and the expectation of embarrassment), indicates that this most creole of their codes is associated with the antisocial, with the motive of challenge to the household value system. This difference of speaking varieties symbolizes a clash of value systems, which I have attempted to demonstrate elsewhere, between male and female segments of the community (Abrahams 1970a). This is a conflict also between the worlds of *being sensible* and *talking nonsense,* of *acting behaved* and *acting rude* (Abrahams and Bauman 1971).

This conflict arises constantly in discussions of men by women and of the young by their elders. This does not mean, however, that nonsense is not appreciated. It has served important social functions within the social system by giving the ones who would act on their rude intentions their time of license. But in one ceremony, the West Indian *tea meeting,* the two worlds and their underlying values are brought into open contest, their values and language varieties counterpoised for purposes of entertainment.

On St. Vincent the organizing idea of the tea meeting is not only to present the most important cultural information (*facts*) about the Gospels or Emancipation in oratorical form, but also to juxtapose the *orators* against the rude *pit boys,* each attempting to confuse the others. This contest motive is regarded as the central feature of the *tea meeting.* As one chairman, Charles Jack, discusses it:

> The pit boys and all that nonsense, that forms part of the enjoyment, the entertainment. Everybody there have their time. You have a time for the chairman, you have a time for the orator, you have a time to say poems and rags and so on. And you have a time to rap, you have a time to get refreshment. You have a time for everything.

Though Mr. Jack here sets forth the contesting elements in terms of each having his *time,* in fact, the forces are constantly contending with each other. Those on the stage, the chairman, choir, and orators, must constantly contend for the attention of the audience against the rude ones who would seize the limelight and confuse the performers. As Mr. Jack pointed out, the primary tactics are through the *rapping* of the *pit boys*—banging sticks on the benches and chairbacks while chanting, usually for the refreshments—and the *ragging,* poems shouted by an audience member making fun of the speaking powers of an orator, through a slur or a boast. The speaker must learn how to respond appropriately—with a countering rhyme or jest, or simply by proceeding strongly. But the contest motive and the attempt to confuse through the use of rudeness and nonsense in ragging is evident throughout.

> The rag will be coming from the others who want to confuse you. I'll tell you the whole thing—it is that you are going on the platform and

> when someone starts ragging you, now, if you're not one who has
> very good memory, you're likely to forget what you had to say. When
> you're going on the platform and you begin saying your speech, now
> you're burst. They could mock you and that is the purpose, the main
> objective of these rhymes. (Charles Jack)[2]

Both the *orators* and those *making mock,* then, are attempting
to confuse the others, and it is this contest of confusion which
provides the major focus of interest. But the orator must
confuse through his command of *facts* and his ability to keep
cool and be *sensible,* while those *ragging* operate with the
strategy of licensed *nonsense* and *rudeness.*

Though the orator has always played an important role in
the tea meeting, he has become more central to the ceremony
within the last twenty-five or thirty years. Before that time,
the major focus of the evening was the speeches of the
chairmen; they were the reference figures for the orators, the
ones not only who trained them but whom they aspired to
emulate and eventually outspeak. But recently the desirability
of learning to speak well has lessened somewhat and thus
incentives have had to be provided by the tea meeting
entrepreneurs to get the scholars to commit themselves to the
ordeal. Thus the chairmen serve as much to bolster the
confidence of the scholars as to exhibit their abilities.

> ... those days, the days when I started, the chairman and
> vice-chairman, secretary had to do a lot of talking, because there was
> no prize meeting in those days. But since we have a prize meeting we
> depend [more] on the judges, because you can say we as chairman,
> vice-chairman, and secretary, we can say as much as we like, but the
> prizes for the children; orators and oratoresses depend upon the
> judges for the morning [when the prizes are announced]. We have
> only to congratulate them. Every three persons that speak, boys or
> girls, the chairman will congratulate such and such a person ... and
> explain to the audience what the children are speaking about. (Clive
> Richardson)

There has been a shift in the focus of the proceedings,
then, in an attempt to keep the young's interest in *talking
sweet,* in speechmaking. This is, of course, one battle in the
war to maintain the family system and household values of the

past. For this reason, parents continue to encourage their children, if they exhibit speaking talent, to learn the tea meeting techniques and to enter into competition. This encouragement takes the form of the parents entering into an agreement with a man of proven oratorical abilities (usually a chairman) to teach speeches to their child. Commonly they will pay him to do this between $3.00 and $10.00 Eastern Caribbean Currency (approximately $1.50 to $5.00 U.S.) depending upon their ability to pay. This is roughly the equivalent of a week's wages.

The man of words teachers conceive of this apprenticeship as a *school* or *college* for *orators, scholars.* They teach by meeting with the entire class (generally five to ten students) about a month before the scheduled tea meeting. Usually these sessions are held on Sundays and the students dress in the church clothes, as they will at the meeting. At that point they will have written out speeches, *lessons*, for each, which the professors will read aloud and discuss in terms of the theory of presentational principles, how to stand, speak loudly and clearly, handle the mockery of the audience, make counter jokes, appropriately flatter the judges, and so on. They will ask the student orators to read them aloud, acting on the principles discussed. The *professor* will judge and comment along the way, correcting pronunciation, enunciation, misplaced emphases, and speaking rhythm. In other words, the professor is charged with the task of teaching not only the speeches but the proper manner of speechmaking, especially in regard to the features which the judges will take into consideration. The criteria of judgment are primarily the manner of delivery, the fluency of speaking, and perhaps most important, the way in which the scholar keeps himself composed and thus is able to manipulate the audience more effectively.

> The judges give a lot according to how the boy and girl are speaking, how they ascend or descend. He must know how to descend, how to lower your voice, and all that comes in when the judges are judging. [They are concerned] not only in the oration alone but how the boy or the girl go about herself on the platform. (Clive Richardson)

The student then is expected to take the lesson home and commit it to memory within the next two weeks. Again they will meet on a Sunday, at which time they will perform for the professor and he will make further comments on their delivery. Usually, at least two and sometimes three sessions of this sort are held, but not always with all of the students present. One student may come to the orator's house in the evening if there is special help needed.

At the end of the schooling just before the meeting, the professor generally goes to the home to hear the speech and to make comments upon it in front of the parents. "I'll call to their mother or father. They will hear their children's conversation. Any mistakes, I try to correct them" (Ledly Jackson).

This process had changed in the recent past because of the growing literacy of the population. In the past the children would have to be taught their lessons by repetition; in some ways, these days are regarded as having been more fulfilling to the professors, for they had a larger part in the training program.

> In some years, if I can remember, I tell you, I carry from here seven—between girls and boys—seven, from here to Kingstown [the capital of St. Vincent, where the meeting was held]. There were seven prizes and carried the whole seven here. And the girl that won the first best prize, I told the judges next morning, "Show her a book and I bet she doesn't know it." And they did and she doesn't know it. They showed it to her and she could never read the alphabet, nothing at all. Those that could not write, you see, I just repeat it over for them and they learn it or I use the strap to you. . . . My children, they must know me victorious that night [of the meeting]. If not, your judges have trouble with me. (Ledly Jackson)

The professor is thus deeply involved in the outcome of the proceedings, viewing the meeting as a contest of wits, a war of words.

> . . . 'Tis said, "There'll be no peace until the battle is ended and the man who'll be victorious will wear the crown." Supposing we had just one prize. I have my speakers, and elsewhere you have yours. You

would like to see that speaker carry home the prize and what do you
think I would like? Well, how can we have peace? (Ledly Jackson)

A professor will gather a following, especially if his scholars
win with any regularity. A good student may come back year
after year to learn new speeches. However, as long as the
orator continues to learn the speeches as they are written out,
he has no chance of ascending to the place of chairman. It is
the underlying structure of the speech which must be
recognized and the willingness to learn to substitute different
content units into the structural slots, thus improving the
orations, that would enable the young man (or, in at least one
case, woman) to outspeak a chairman and to oust him from his
position. As may be imagined, this usurpation occurs very
rarely, but each chairman has a personal legend (often
performed by him in informal gatherings) in which he recounts
the occasion on which he ascended to a chairmanship.

As with any other involved and improvised verbal form,
the training of the man of words in talking sweet for tea
meeting involves teaching him a repertoire of clichés and
commonplaces, or "formulas" as the followers of Parry and
Lord's methodology call them (Lord 1960). At the beginning
of the training, these nonmetrical formulaic devices are
embodied in the set speech written out by the professor as a
lesson. As the orator progresses, however, he will begin to
recognize that certain kinds of clichés are appropriate to
certain parts of the speech, and that he may substitute if he
cares to. It is when he has learned a large number of these and
has developed the ability to improvise (perhaps making up or
developing from books some runs of his own) that he begins to
think of challenging the chairman.

There are essentially three sections of the oration: the
address, the *speech* (also called the *topic* or *doctrine* of the
body of the speech), and the *joke.* The speech is the central
portion and takes the greatest amount of time. The judges will
be primarily concerned with this section because this is where
the demonstration of knowledge, of talking sensibly and
factually, will arise. The younger orators, in fact, are taught

only this section and a very quick, one-line *joke,* for if they do nothing else, they must demonstrate the wisdom of their professors.

The first section, then, the *address,* is the optional one, but it is also the one which, when fully developed, leads to becoming chairman, for it involves the same kind of elaborate compliments and macaronic diction which the chairman must demonstrate. The major focus of the *address* is the ritual compliment, which may be addressed to the chairmen, the judges, the choir leader (*Mr. Presenter*) or to members of the audience.

> Pleasant evening to these lovely ladies, also to these honorable gentlemen, admitting Mr. Presenter and his choir. Charming ladies. Mr. Chairman, sir, whilst I was sitting in yonder corner, gazing on these *quorum nobis* young ladies with their silver laces and magnificent brooches, they were as bright as the wonderful star that led the wise men from the east into Bethlehem. Charming ladies!! (bows).

This address, which is one from what we might call an intermediate scholar, is comparatively bare of the eloquent flourishes which characterize the *addresses* of the accomplished orator.

> Mr. Chairman, judges, ladies and gentlemen, I feel totally ineducate to expiate upon a question so momentously to ourselves. It would be happy and necessary for Africa and the East, for I will be able to express myself before thee. And it is with privilege, hearing my name being called, I stand before you on this rostrum. Chairmen, ladies, and gentlemen, the grandeur of this meeting fills my mind with job and remitting felicity and, like Alexander the Great when he having manifest his vicinity at Alexandria and thus explain in the language Athenian, *careto claret primus disjecta membera* of the festivity. But let us please to remember that your Demosthenes *astronema* is here, whose intellectual faculty knows no bounds. Seated in the accidental corner of your rostrum, chairmen, listening to the copious *andoy op dos artac canum nobis,* so it is with concordial *crescentenana felices maniam que dices que*[3] *quaniam, pacito el picallo gabito quanto.* I have the privilege of arising before this rostrum to give my conversation. As in my lover's lap lying [much laughter], hearing, hearing my name so widely called by your secretary who writes *carenti calemor.* And so it is with great *viventi,* due *viventi, duos*

levitii, that I have arisen to vindicate my call, and to let the vindicators of my evincitation be known. (Ledly Jackson)

The *address* and the *joke,* which serve as framing elements for the *speech,* rely on a combination of erudition and humor, both being presented in as dramatically elaborated a manner as possible (as is made clear by the hypercareful enunciation by the most successful orators at these points). But the hyperbole of the address is commonly directed toward others, while that of the joke takes on a boasting form. One of the continuing features of the speech is the heightening of dramatic effect at the end of a passage by the statement, "Tracing on a little further," or the question, "Mr. Chairman, must I proceed?" The concluding joke, too, begins with this question and always turns on some absurd reason why the orator must not continue because of the dire calamities which would ensue:

> No, I will not, for if I continue these beautiful young ladies will fall on me just like the Falls of Niagara. No, if I go on I will break down the stage, leaving none for the common orators. Under these circumstances, I will not continue, but I will take my congratulations, for I am an orator.
> > Once my enemy did attempt to run
> > But shot and powder has recalled them back to me.
> > But if these beasts had dared to run,
> > I'll bring them back with machine gun.
> So adieu.

But, as mentioned, the major portion of the oration is the *speech.* This is always a direct quotation from a book (or books) chosen because the content is appropriate to the *season.* This may mean, from the Euro-American perspective, that a passage seems to begin in mid-argument:

> Mr. Chairman, sir, my doctrine I will now inform you of is about Emancipation. [Emancipation, thank you.] Ladies and gentlemen, but while Mr. Clarkson formed a rich reward for his past labors, in the success which crowned his efforts, his triumph animated him for his new exertions. On the month he found himself elevated, he saw the horizon widen, and bright were his hopes for the future. When he

said, "But independently of the quantity of physical suffering innumerable abuse to vice in more than a quarter of the globe."

Ladies and gentlemen. We have reasons to consider, as like you to permit. Mr. Chairman, sir, we have this great probability that Africa now free from the vicious and barbarous effect of this traffic may be in a better state to comprehend and receive the sublime truths of the Christian religion. [Fact, Fact.[4]]

The ideal of the *sweet talk* man of words, whether an orator or a chairman, is to go *higher* than the other speakers. *High* means not only to ascend the heights of rhetorical inventiveness but to speak long and copiously. This means that the first two of the three sections will grow by the addition of compliments and greater portions of memorized text. When this occurs, it becomes necessary to break these sections into smaller units, giving clear enunciation to the beginning of the new unit. This is done generally in the address by having a formulaic series of comparisons with great men, and in the speech, by beginning each section with a renewed address or with the addition of the call for the question of whether the speaker shall proceed. Here, as an example, is a speech given by an advanced student:

Address
Mr. Chairman, fellow citizens, ladies and gentlemen, including these ceremonial judges. Admitting Mr. Presenter and choir. Wishing the audience a happy and joyful evening.

Mr. Presenter, sir, while listening to yourself and choir, I think it was Mr. Tennyson's choir singing in the St. Paul's Cathedral. Then sir, to whom must I compare you? I must compare you to the great man George Fredrick Handel, now, the German composer. You are greater. I must now compare you to Admiral Collingwood, Lord Nelson's second in command at Trafalgar. He was born in 1750. He completed his excellence of Cape St. Vincent in 1797. As for you, Mr. Chairman, it is in island spread that you are a Biblical and classical presiding officer. Then sir, to whom must I compare you? I must now compare you to that great man John Ephilopótus who reckon the first King Syria after Alexander the Great. (Thank you.)

Speech
Mr. Chairman, ladies and gentlemen. I dare not close this chapter without repeating what I have said on this occasion. Those who fought for the freedom of their slaves performed their duty heroically, while but their duties still remained for those so early.

Your honor the judge, you know in the economy of God, there is one standard pathway for these races, by beginning at the bottom and gradually climbing to the highest possibilities of his nature. He will send in the years to come, the help, the guidance, the encouragement that the strong convey to the weak.

Ladies and gentlemen, may I proceed? [Proceed] Mr. Chairman sir, must I continue? [Continue] My evening doctrine is about emancipation. Ladies and gentlemen, in chapter fifteen, page 179, "Freedom Declared in Antigua in 1834, in Jamaica in 1838." The Negroes continued most orderly, oppressive measure of some planters. The gradual improvement of the freed men. The committee of the Antigua Legislature reported: "We do not, we confess, discover any sufficient reason in the island, why an honorous and strict emancipation should not answer as well as in 1834 as in 1838 or 1840." The consequence of this report was such that this emancipation was there proclaimed without the intervention of the mistaken system of apprenticeship.

Chairmen, ladies. Though that system was proposed as a precautionary step it was certainly grounded on many ignorant and imaginary fears of the Negro character which was supposed to the people in Antigua to be a bold and most successful experiment.

Joke
Mr. Chairman, sir, must I continue? [Continue] No, I will not for there is someone else behind whose head's hot, whose heart swelling, just as a rosebud swell and burst out in the month of May listening for the voice of his sweetheart.

As mentioned, the task of the professor goes beyond simply teaching the speeches. Fluency, diction, and most important, audience command is emphasized. The student orators are taught that they must tread the very fine line between *confusing* (amazing) the audience, by using long words and leading them into the special kind of active receptiveness characteristic of Afro-American performances, and confusing them too much and thus losing their interest.

According to how high is your language, they [the audience] may not understand it. . . . Of course, you'll be talking to a mixed audience, some more educated than you, like the judges, and some less. And in that mixed audience, if you go too high, some couldn't be able to understand you; if you go too low, some will underestimate you. So you have to meet all the sections of your audience. (Charles Jack)

One must learn as well how to handle a mistake in the speechmaking:

> If you're talking along, and, for example, you make a mistake, rather than repeating yourself so that those who know will understand that you have made an error, give a joke right there. Or else, turn to the chairman, "Mr. Chairman, must I continue?" and so on, "Your honor, the judges, must I ejaculate?" Well they'll answer you and say "Well, ejaculate," or "Continue" as the case may be. And it give you time to pick up. You must be able to do that at intervals. . . . Or you might say "Look, well, I'm going to recite a little poem" and that might work. (Charles Jack)

The important feature, stressed again and again in the professional teachings, is mental and verbal agility.

> . . . the moment decides and you have to be a fast thinker. And when you are in control, you must be able to know to think fast, what to do, how to do it, so that nobody vexed with you. And you get your call back [assent from the chairmen or the judges to proceed]. If they're vexed with you, you know, they'll start to heckle you. And when you start getting heckling, well you know the confusion. And when they confuse you, you know, that will mean the end of the speaking. (Charles Jack)

But the answer for confusion may simply be inaction and silence, for this too means maintaining one's sense of the cool.

> The boys of Richland Park, they would rhyme the boys at Evesham [two villages in the Mesopotamian Valley] . . . when they are ascending the platform. . . . They are trying to confuse them. They can sometimes make a joke back or sometimes just stand upon the platform for two or three minutes. When the rhyming is finished, then they can get to themselves . . . and they can carry on. (Clive Richardson)

That confusion and contest rule this occasion is important in an understanding of why this ceremony has developed. This uproarious meeting differs from similar occasions for eloquence in European and Euro-American cultures because of the various attempts made to "confuse." The battle of wits is so organized because the Vincentian would see little value in the demonstration of the coolness (or lack of confusion) of the orator if it were not tested, contested, surrounded by a heated-up audience. Though the speeches are calculated to obtain the attention of the audience, attention does not mean quiet. In fact, if the speaker is not able to obtain the "hot" responses of laughter, rapping, clapping, and continuative words (like "fact, fact" or "proceed), he regards his performance as a failure. And well he must, because the alternatives to this guided response are louder noises, generally of a derisive nature. Thus, learning to *talk sweet* is calculated not just to show an ability to speak a variety of English effectively; far more important, it provides an occasion to perform, edify, entertain, and demonstrate, through the esthetic of the cool, the highest values of the group. By this, the group and the performing individuals achieve a sense of fulfillment—the group because it has come together and celebrated its overt values, and the individual because his abilities have been utilized and tested in a manner that allows him to achieve status.

NOTES

1. Material for this paper was gathered during two field trips, one in spring, 1966, when a fellow of the John Simon Guggenheim Foundation, the other in the summer of 1968 while on an NIMH Small Grant, MH 15706-01, "Stereotype and Prejudice Maintenance in the British West Indies." I am indebted to many for their critical examination of this paper, especially Dell Hymes.

2. This and the following are quotations from interviews held with the principal chairmen-professors on the island, recorded in August 1968.

3. Reasonably accurate orthography is difficult here because the orator begins to alternate between Latin and Spanish allusions.

4. This interjection is not only an approving continuative, but an indication to the judges that "truth" has been given voice and should be borne in mind in the judging.

REFERENCES CITED

Abrahams, Roger D.
    1970a   The Black Uses of Black English. Unpublished MS.
    1970b   The West Indian Tea Meeting and Afro-American Expressive
              Culture. Unpublished MS.
Abrahams, Roger D. and Bauman, Richard
    1971   Sense and Nonsense in St. Vincent. American Anthropologist
              73:762-772.
Lord, Albert B.
    1960   The Singer of Tales. Cambridge, Massachusetts: Harvard University
              Press.
Wilson, Peter J.
    1969   Reputation and Respectability: Suggestions for Caribbean
              Ethnology. Man 4:70-84.

10

CUNA IKALA:
Literature in San Blas*

Joel F. Sherzer

The Cuna Indians live on island and mainland communities off the Atlantic coast of Panama near the border with Colombia, as well as along the Bayano and Chucunaque rivers in the interior jungle area of Panama. This paper reports mainly on the first group, the coastal San Blas Cuna.[1] The Cuna have a rich tradition of speaking and chanting which is intimately related to their social, political, religious, and medical life. An important aspect of this tradition is the existence of a variety of ceremonial and ritual linguistic varieties, in addition to the colloquial. Beyond its important role in sociocultural life, Cuna speaking and chanting can be viewed in and for itself as verbal art (literature).

*I would like to dedicate this paper to the memory of Olowitinappi, *arkar, inatulet,* and *ikar wisit* of Sasardi-Mulatupo, who died on April 20, 1975. Olowitinappi's extensive knowledge was well known in San Blas. He served as informant for portions of this paper.

The Cuna word *ikala* (or *ikar*) can mean "adventure, custom, journey, lesson, path, way." We can also use it to refer to "literature,"[2] as long as a distinction is made between "Western" literature and Cuna literature. For a Western audience literature usually signifies a body of masterpieces that a few educated people are able to read and enjoy. Cuna verbal art on the other hand is an instrumental part of various aspects of Cuna life; for example, curing, greeting, and social control. It so happens that the texts used for these and other purposes are quite clearly considered by the Cuna themselves not only to be different from the everyday or colloquial language, but to be special and indeed artistic or esthetically pleasing. There is much evidence for this.

First, people talk of good and bad performers, using criteria that have to do with such artistic properties of performances as loudness of voice, amount of knowledge displayed, and type of content. Bad performers may still perform the social roles of curing, greeting, social control, etc.; but they are much less appreciated from the point of view of artistic verbal ability. Good performers, on the other hand, will be paid to perform, even if the social role is not involved, by patrons appreciating the purely artistic aspects of the performance. This is quite common during the festivities associated with girls' puberty rites, when all members of the community take the day off and get drunk. As entertainment for the occasion they often pay a good performer to chant a curing *ikar,* although of course no curing is involved. Furthermore, there are various schools or traditions of performance in San Blas and in the nearby jungle. These traditions differ not in the social purposes for which they are used but rather in the actual textual material. They differ in their verbal artistic properties. It is possible and proper then, from the native Cuna point of view, to label Cuna *ikala* "literature," as long as the social role is not lost sight of.

I will deal with three aspects of Cuna literature: (1) the microstructure of literary texts—the texture of the texts; (2) the macrostructure of literary texts—the content of the texts and the classification of literary genres; (3) the role of literature in culture and society.

Microstructure

Sociolinguistic repertoire and its relationship to literature

There are many varieties within the Cuna sociolinguistic system. The relationship among these varieties is one of the most fascinating aspects of Cuna linguistics and literature. The Cuna themselves recognize the different varieties as appropriate to or belonging to various colloquial and ceremonial traditions. Some examples are the *historical-political-religious* tradition, the *curing* tradition, the *kantule* or *chicha festival* tradition, the *storytelling* or *kwento* tradition, the *purpa* or *sekretto* tradition, and the *arkar* or *interpreter* tradition. It is thus necessary to specify the relationship not between the colloquial and a single poetic or verbal art variety, but between the colloquial and several ceremonial varieties and verbal traditions. The linguistic characteristics of the various ceremonial varieties are not totally distinct from one another. Instead, there is an overlapping of phonological, syntactic, and semantic systems forming a total system, which includes the colloquial and the ceremonial varieties. I will illustrate this situation here by means of examples, first from phonology and then from the lexicon. (Discussion of parallelism below further illustrates the richness of the Cuna sociolinguistic system.)

In the colloquial language there is typically a great deal of vowel elision, bringing together consonants that in turn undergo changes. For example underlying

1) *walappa* "three pole-like objects" becomes by vowel elision
2) *walppaa* and by consonantal changes
3) *warpaa.*

Form (3) is common in colloquial speech. Form (2) is never used, in any variety. Form (1) is used in colloquial speech for rhetorical emphasis, for example when insisting or when angry.

It is also used in storytelling and speechmaking for emphasis. It is most common in historical-political-religious, curing, and chicha festival texts. This example is representative of the role of vowel elision in colloquial and ceremonial varieties of Cuna. It is important to point out that elision does not always occur in colloquial speech. It does not operate when rhetorical emphasis is intended. Nor does elision always fail to operate in the ceremonial varieties; it is however much more common in these. Vowel lengthening as an expressive device parallels the absence of elision with regard to function in colloquial and ceremonial speech; i.e., lengthened vowels are used in colloquial speech primarily for rhetorical emphasis and are much more common in ceremonial speech.

From this phonological example it should be clear that it would be quite incorrect to say that forms in Cuna poetic or verbally artistic varieties are in any sense deviations from forms in colloquial speech.[3] Rather there is an intimate relationship between colloquial and ceremonial speech according to which one phonological possibility sometimes exploited in colloquial speech (the underlying form) takes precedence in ceremonial speech. The Cuna consider the ceremonial varieties, which conserve their traditions, as in some sense more archaic than the colloquial. It is thus interesting that the more conservative Cuna dialects of the Darien jungle tend to have much less vowel elision, even in everyday, colloquial speech.[4]

In the area of the lexicon the situation is somewhat different. Each variety has certain lexical items particular to it. Some lexical items are shared by several varieties. Thus, the word for woman is *ome* in colloquial speech, *tuttu* (which in colloquial speech means "flower") in historical-political-religious chants, and *walepunkwa* (which has no meaning in colloquial speech) in curing *ikar*. Sometimes the difference between the forms used in colloquial and ceremonial speech involves prefixes or suffixes particular to ceremonial but not colloquial varieties. Thus *kachi* "hammock" is *pokachi* in the historical-political-religious chants and *ipepokachipilli* in some of the curing *ikar*. Certain areas of vocabulary especially, certain semantic fields, tend to have distinct lexical realizations in the different linguistic varieties. These are animals and plants, body parts, celestial bodies, color terms, kinship terms, and natural elements. It seems worthwhile to point out that lexical switching does not suffice in itself to define or mark a poetic form. Lexical switching also occurs within the colloquial variety, serving sociocultural functions other than the poetic. A striking example involves a number of animals and plants that have distinct names for use at night. It is believed that the use of the day name at night can be dangerous for various reasons—the hunted animal might be warned, the animal or plant in question might be aroused and cause trouble, etc. The Cuna do not view these night names as verbally artistic, but rather as socially necessary.[5] Table 1 provides examples showing the nature of the lexical relationship among some Cuna varieties.

Parallelism

As in much verbal art around the world (see Jakobson 1968) parallelism is a major principle of Cuna verbal art. In Cuna literature, parallelism enables the performer to make texts very long, therefore effective and artistic at the same time (from the Cuna point of view). One important generating principle behind Cuna parallelistic structures is the interplay of ceremonial and colloquial linguistic varieties. Since parallelism can often be viewed (again following Jakobson) as the projection of the paradigmatic onto the syntagmatic, our task as analysts is to uncover both the paradigms and the principles of syntagmatic projection. I will illustrate this here with three different Cuna *ikar,* all in the genre: curing.

pisep ikar

pisep ikar "the way of the *pisep*" is used in the hunting of wild animals in the jungle. The hunter bathes in a potion made from the fragrant *pisep* plant and has *pisep ikar* performed for him by a specialist. The following portion of *pisep ikar* deals with the birth (symbolically described) of the *pisep* plant.

Table 1

English	Cuna colloquial		historical-political-religious[6]	curing[6]	animal stories[7]
	day	night			
"rabbit"	sule	nappanono "head in earth"	olopurwakkilele		ulukkatturkipanaler
"snail"	salu	tios uaya "god's ears"			
"devilfish"	nitirpi		olopyokkilele		oloparpalikinya
"alligator"	tain		oloarwaliele	kilu ulu sai ipekan	inapurtikapaler
"knife"	esa			ipetintuli	
"hammock"	kachi		pokachi	ipepokachipilli	
"eye"	ipya			tala	
"throat"	kammu		kolowala "calling pole"	kolowala	
"woman"	ome		tuttu "flower"	walepunkwa	
"Spaniard, Panamanian"	waka		tulepiitti	pilatola	

inapiseptili	*oloulu ti tulalemaiye*
	olouliti tulallemaiye
inapiseptili	*oloulu ti sikkirmakkemaiye*
	oloulu ti sikkirmakmamaiye
inapiseptili	*oloulu ti wawanmakkemaiye*
	oloulu ti wawanmakmainaye
inapiseptili	*oloulu ti aktutumakkemaiye*
	oloulu ti aktutulemainaye
inapiseptili	*oloulu ti kollomakkemaiye*
	oloulu ti kollomakmainaye
inapiseptili	*oloulu ti mummurmakkemaiye*
	oloulu ti mummurmakmainaye

the pisep plant, in the golden box, is moving
in the golden box, is moving
the pisep plant, in the golden box, is swinging from side to side
in the golden box, is swinging from side to side
the pisep plant, in the golden box, is trembling
in the golden box, is trembling
the pisep plant, in the golden box, is palpitating
in the golden box, is palpitating
the pisep plant, in the golden box, is making a noise
in the golden box, is making a noise
the pisep plant, in the golden box, is shooting out
in the golden box, is shooting out

It is possible to represent this text in the form of a series of symbols. The symbolic representation renders the operation of the principle of parallelism much more striking. The symbols are:

a: pisep plant
b: golden box
c, d, e, f, g, h: various verb stems
W, w: makke, mak: verb stem ending
x: mai: verbal suffix "in the process of"
y: na: verbal suffix "movement to a particular location"
z: ye: verbal suffix "subjunctive"

The text can now be rewritten as:

a	b	c		x		z		a	b	f	W	x		z
	b	c		x		z			b	f		x	y	z
a	b	d	W	x		z		a	b	g	W	x		z
	b	d	w	x	x	z			b	g	w	x	y	z
a	b	e	W	x		z		a	b	h	W	x		z
	b	e	w	x	y	z			b	h	w	x	y	z

The above representation shows that the text is based on a complex overlapping of parallelistic structures. There are, for example, the repetition of the pattern:

a   b
      b;

the coupled repetition   c   d   e   f   g   h
                         c   d   e   f   g   h;

the 12-fold repetition of x . . . z.

The parallelism draws on the interplay between colloquial Cuna and the ceremonial variety characteristic of curing *ikar*. Thus the repeated nominal affixes *olo . . . ti* are from the curing variety. The verbal suffixes *-na* (y), which in colloquial Cuna signifies "movement to a particular location," and *-ye* (z), which in colloquial Cuna has subjunctive-like force, lose much of their referential meaning in *pisep ikar* and function mainly as ceremonial adornments and fillers. Verbs *d* through *h* terminate in the verbal stem ending *-makke*. *-makke* has two forms—a long, ceremonial form *-makke* (W) and a short, colloquial form *-mak* (w). In this portion of *pisep ikar* the long and short forms, the ceremonial and the colloquial, are alternated in a verbal pattern: Ww, Ww, etc. Notice that this alternation does not indicate a constant shift from a ceremonial to a colloquial genre; rather the resources of the Cuna sociolinguistic system, which includes ceremonial and colloquial forms, are drawn on in the creation of the parallelistic structures of this ceremonial genre.

kurkin ikar

kurkin ikar "the way of the hat" is used in the curing of headaches. The portion represented here deals with the great strength of trees that will do the curing in the form of stick dolls addressed by the perfomer of the *ikar*.

> *kurkin ipe*kan [ti] [ye] [olo] pillise *pupawal(a)*kan akku(e)kwic(i) [ye]
> "trees, your roots reach the level of gold"

> *kurkin ipe*kan [ti] [ye] [olo] pillise pe maliwaskakan upo(e)kwic(i) [ye]
> "trees, your small roots are placed into the level of gold"

*kurkin ipe*kan [ti] [na] [ye] [olo] pillise pe maliwaskakan(a) piokle
[ke] kwic(i) [ye]
"trees, your small roots are nailed into the level of gold"

*kurkin ipe*kan [ti] [na] [ye] [olo] pillipi [ye] ap(i)ka(e)kwic(i) [ye]
"trees, within the very level of god you are resisting"

Again, the parallelistic repetition is characteristic of this *ikar*. Thus, in every line is repeated "trees, level of gold." Also, the resources provided by both colloquial and ceremonial varieties are drawn on. This is shown in the text by italicizing lexical items used only in this genre and bracketing affixes characteristic of the linguistic variety of curing. In this *ikar* (as in others) lines are repeated with verbs of slightly differing meaning or perspective, resulting in a slowly developing sequence, not unlike one aspect of the French *nouveau roman*.

kapur ikar

kapur ikar "the way of the hot pepper" is used in the curing of high fever. The portion of *kapur ikar* discussed here names and thus controls different types of *kapur* "hot pepper," which are used in the actual curing process. The curing variety of Cuna provides a much more complete and elaborate taxonomy for hot pepper than colloquial Cuna (in addition to each member of the taxonomy having a name in the ceremonial variety different from the colloquial). We can view the taxonomy provided by the curing variety (a taxonomy which includes 55 types of hot pepper) as a "ceremonial paradigm"; in this portion of *kapur ikar* this ceremonial paradigm is projected or mapped onto a single verse pattern, thus producing 55 parallel verses, differing only in the type of hot pepper named. This situation is represented below, in which a, b, c, etc. are types of *kapur* and x, y, z, q are subtypes. The taxonomy or "ceremonial paradigm" is drawn on and mapped onto the verse pattern by moving from top to bottom and from left to right—first *kapur* itself, then a, then x under a, then y under a, then z under a, then q under a, then b, then x under b, then y under b, etc. Thus

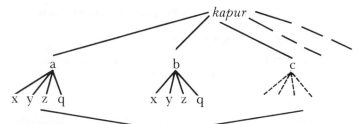

in the north	the flowers are perceived
name of *kapur*	the leaves are perceived
name of type of *kapur*	the stems are perceived
name of subtype of *kapur*	the seeds are perceived
is named	

This example, like the other two, shows how Cuna ceremonial language (in this case the linguistic variety of curing) is drawn on in the creation of parallelistic patterns. As can be seen from the texts discussed here, Cuna parallelism involves many and multiple repetitions. The resulting verbal events are extremely long and slow moving from the referential point of view. For the Cuna, length is a marker of verbal art and of a performer's ability—it is by means of lack of vowel elision, added morphological and syntactic material, literal slowness of delivery, and parallelism that this length is achieved.

Macrostructure

Classification of literary genres

Because of the intimate relationship between Cuna verbal art and sociocultural life, a classification of literary genres is at the same time a classification of sociocultural events, at least those in which speaking and chanting are central, and these are many. It is clear then that a classification of literary genres is impossible on the basis of internal linguistic structure alone, but rather we must go beyond the texts and investigate the contexts in which they occur. To do so, I make use of the factors or components of speech (see Jakobson 1960; Hymes 1962,. 1972) which relate language and speech (in this case Cuna verbal art) to their contexts of use.[8] The classification is shown in Table 2. It makes use of the following components of speech—*setting, variety, channel, sender, receiver, audience,* and *purpose.*

Notice that in the classification shown in Table 2 *purpose* is always listed in terms of primary, sociocultural purpose. As mentioned above, Cuna *ikar* "texts" are often performed for secondary purposes as well. Thus, curing *ikar*, whose primary purpose is the curing of disease, can also be performed for the secondary purposes of learning, teaching, practicing, showing off, pure pleasure (of both performer and listener, as at festivities associated with girls' puberty rites), etc. In the performance of *ikar* for these secondary purposes, other components of speech may vary as well. Thus, when performing a curing *ikar* for teaching, the *wisit* "knower" or "specialist" is usually in his own house; the channel is *namakke* "chanted" rather than *sunmakke* "spoken."[10] These different purposes for which the same *ikar* may be performed and the different ways (in terms of the components of speech) in which the performance occurs, may be conceived of as different *frames* for *ikar* performance (frame being used here as in Goffman 1974). The rich variety of frames in which single *ikar* can be performed is evidence of the vitality of Cuna literature in particular and Cuna sociocultural life in general.

Productivité

It is instructive to consider the content of Cuna literature from a perspective proposed by Julia Kristeva (1968). Kristeva writes" "Le texte est une *productivité* ... il est une permutation de textes, une intertextualité: dans l'espace d'un texte plusieurs énoncés pris à d'autres textes se croisent et se neutralisent" (299). "Considérons les différentes séquences (ou codes) d'une structure textuelle précise comme autant de 'transforms' de séquences (de codes) prises à d'autres textes" (311).

Table 2

Text	Setting	Variety	Channel
historical-political-religious	congress house	"congress" language	chanted
arkar "chief's spokesman" interpretation; speechmaking	congress house	speechmaking style	spoken
arkan kae "ceremonial greeting"	congress house	"congress" language	chanted
uanaet "advice to individuals who have misbehaved, newly married couples, village officials, etc.	congress house	speechmaking style	spoken
curing and related *ikar*	sick person's house, other appropriate locations	"stick doll" language	spoken
kantule or *chicha* festival *ikar*	*chicha* house	*kantule's* language	shouted
purpa or *sekretto* "secrets"	in sender's house or place where object in question is found	charmlike language[9] specific to object to be controlled	spoken
animal and plant stories	congress house (usually)	colloquial Cuna, with animal and plant names specific to story	spoken
lullabies	house of baby, in hammock	colloquial Cuna	chanted

Table 2 (continued)

Sender	Receiver	Audience	Purpose
chief	another chief	men and women present	social control
arkar, speech maker	village officials, men/women present	men/women present	social control, reports, discussion, village problems
visiting chief / host chief	{ host chief / visiting chief }	anyone present	greeting between two chiefs for their respective villages
chief/*arkar*	person(s) being advised	men/women present	social control
wisit "knower" of *ikar*	stick dolls, other relevant objects	persons present	cure disease, control objects, etc.
kantule	*kammu* "flute"	those present	narrate and aid in hair-cutting rite occurring elsewhere at same time
knower of "secret"	object to be controlled	none	control object
story teller, often chief or *arkar*	one person, who asks questions and makes comments	those present	entertainment
older female relative of baby	baby	those present	put baby to sleep

An investigation of Cuna *ikala* often reveals elements borrowed from other *ikala,* past and recent history, as well as personal experiences, transformed and incorporated into a single text. Such texts are thus *productivités* in the sense of Kristeva. Examples can be drawn from the various genres of Cuna literature. The medicinal curing *ikar* describe long battles which the *suar mimmi* "stick dolls" must fight against the spirits of sickness. As pointed out by Kramer (1970) these spirits of sickness are transformations of the Spaniards of the sixteenth century who fought wars against the Cuna. The real warfare of the sixteenth century is transformed into the symbolic warfare of the curing *ikar*. *Pap ikala* is a historical-political-religious text that describes life in the afterworld. In *pap ikala* aspects of life in Panama—trains, telephones, elevators, etc.—are incorporated into the description of the Cuna afterworld. Thus the personal experiences of the many Cuna men who when young go to work in Panama are transformed into the content of this *ikar*. *Tatkan ikala* is a historical-political-religious text that recounts Cuna history, both past and recent. When a chief returns from a trip he may use *tatkan ikala* to chant his experiences in the congress house. These experiences include the details of the trip and what he learned from others where he went. The transformed experiences are posed as models and suggestions of the proper way to live. The chief may or may not also communicate this information to others at other times in colloquial Cuna. But its appearance in *tatkan ikala,* chanted in the historical-political-religious variety and used primarily for social control, is an example *par excellence* of transformation and *productivité*. Traditional lullabies, chanted by women to their babies, describe how their husbands are off to work and will soon be back. Into this genre are transformed the particular type of work that the men happen to be doing at the moment—planting corn, cutting bananas, etc.

Thus the concept of *productivité* enables us to view Cuna literature not as a finished and static product but rather as an ongoing and dynamic one. The constant incorporation of new, relevant elements into Cuna *ikala*[11] is not to be mistaken as a sign of acculturation and the demise of a more traditional culture; rather it is an indication of a dynamic and very much alive culture. The processes described here are probably quite old features of the Cuna literary tradition.

Literature in Culture and Society

Under the rubric "literature in culture and society" two rather different though related interpretations are possible:

1) The study of the integration of literature or verbal art and its use in society. This is what most of this paper has been about, investigating Cuna verbal art from the perspectives of sociolinguistics and the ethnography of speaking. Table 2 schematizes the relationship between Cuna verbal art and its use.[12]

2) The study of various aspects of culture in relative isolation from one another to determine if they have similar underlying patterns or structures. Kramer (1970) takes this second approach to Cuna literature in his Chapter III: "Literature in Culture and Society." He compares Cuna literature with Cuna visual art (the colorful *molas* "blouses" made and worn by women) and Cuna music (the playing of panpipes). He argues that just as structural parallelism and repetition is the basic theme of Cuna literature, it is paramount in the other art forms. Though Kramer's presentation is extremely brief and would have benefited from a much more detailed description of the art and music, it does seem to be the case that parallelism and repetition with variation play an important role in the various Cuna art forms. The concept of *productivité,* which was applied above to Cuna literature, operates also in *molas.* The designs of *molas* may be nonrepresentational and geometric or they may represent local animals and plants or objects of everyday use. But other themes are also common, such as Panamanian political campaigns, world boxing matches, religious and festive decorations (angels, crosses, Santa Claus, etc.). The latter are

transformed into the same formats and patterns as the *molas* with more local and native themes—the parallelism and repetition are just as evident. The *molas,* like the *ikala,* involve an ongoing *productivité.*

This brief investigation of Cuna verbal art has aimed at demonstrating on the one hand the inherent richness of Cuna literature and on the other the importance of studying Cuna verbal art in the context of Cuna sociocultural life. I hope to have shown that with regard to such internal linguistic, textual properties as phonological, morphological, syntactic, and lexical patterning and parallelism, Cuna literature is as challenging as the "high" published verbal art of literate societies. At the same time, because of the constant and intimate relationship between Cuna *ikala* and the contexts of its use in Cuna social life, no investigation of Cuna verbal art can stop arbitrarily at the limits of texts.

NOTES

1. Research for this paper was carried out during several field trips among the Cuna, supported by NSF USDP grant GU-1598 to the University of Texas and a small NIMH grant to the author. An earlier version of some of the ideas presented here appeared in Sherzer and Sherzer 1972, which was a review of Kramer 1970. I would like to thank Richard Bauman and Dina Sherzer for many useful discussions.

2. In this paper I also use *ikala* more or less interchangably with "text," since one possible meaning of *ikala* corresponds roughly to what English labels "text."

3. For this view, I refer the reader to Kramer 1970. Of course, and unfortunately, beyond the Cuna, approaches to literary language in terms of deviation remain popular.

4. Patricia Baptista and Ruth Wallin; personal communication.

5. The degree to which these rules for use of day and night names are observed among contemporary Cuna differs from village to village and from individual to individual.

6. Even within varieties there is lexical switching. Thus distinct historical-political-religious chants may have distinct lexical items, as may distinct curing *ikar.* There

are also differences according to geographical and personal traditions. Thus, Table 1 is but a brief sample of the complexity of Cuna lexical switching.

7. In animal stories also there are often several different names for the same animal.

8. See Sherzer 1974 for another classification of Cuna ways of speaking.

9. The *sekrettos* are usually extremely short, meaningless combinations of words, combining Cuna and other languages, for example, Choco, English, and/or Spanish.

10. See Sherzer 1974 for a more complete discussion of various varieties, channels, purposes, etc. of Cuna speech.

11. Some genres are more open than others to the incorporation of new material.

12. See Sherzer 1974 for more on the relationship between Cuna language, culture, and society.

REFERENCES CITED

Goffman, Erving
  1974   Frame Analysis: An Essay on the Organization of Experience. New York: Harper Colophon.

Hymes, Dell
  1962   The Ethnography of Speaking. *In* Anthropology and Human Behavior. T. Gladwin and W. C. Sturtevant, Eds. Washington, D.C.: Anthropological Society of Washington.
  1972   Models of the Interaction of Language and Social Life. *In* Directions in Sociolinguistics. John J. Gumperz and Dell Hymes, Eds. New York: Holt, Rinehart and Winston.

Jakobson, Roman
  1960   Linguistics and Poetics. *In* Style in Language. Thomas A. Sebeok, Ed. Cambridge, Massachusetts: Massachusetts Institute of Technology Press.
  1968   Poetry of Grammar and Grammar of Poetry. Lingua 21:597-609.

Kramer, Fritz
  1970   Literature among the Cuna Indians. Göteborg: Göteborgs Etnografiska Museum, Etnologiska Studier 30.

Kristeva, Julia
  1968   Problèmes de la structuration du texte. *In* Théorie d'ensemble. Paris: Seuil.

Sherzer, Dina and Sherzer, Joel
  1972   Literature in San Blas: Discovering the Cuna *Ikala*. Semiotica 6:182-199.

Sherzer, Joel
  1974   *Namakke, Sunmakke, Kormakke*: Three Types of Cuna Speech Event. *In* Explorations in the Ethnography of Speaking. Richard Bauman and Joel Sherzer, Eds. New York: Cambridge University Press.